The Intercessor's Companion

Bible Ammo to Win Your Battle

Lee Ann Rubsam

Full Gospel Family Publications
Appleton, Wisconsin

The Intercessor's Companion:
Bible Ammo to Win Your Battle

Other Publications:

River Life: Entering into the Character of Jesus
Hotline to Heaven: Hearing the Voice of God
Character Building for Families, Volume 1
Character Building for Families, Volume 2
House of Prayer ~ House of Power
Encouragement from God's Word
How to Pray and Read the Bible
The Beginning Intercessor
God's Word on Healing
The Intercessor Manual
The Names of God

Full Gospel Family Publications
419 East Taft Avenue
Appleton, Wisconsin 54915
FullGospelFamily.com
(920) 734-6693

Table of Contents

Appendices:

Introduction

Intercession is a work of faith, and some of the things we carry before the Lord in prayer challenge our faith extraordinarily. That is why I have written *The Intercessor's Companion* -- to strengthen your faith and to help you stand your ground firmly, so that you receive the answers for which you are laboring.

We begin this book by establishing through Scripture that God truly guides us in what we hear and in how we pray those things through, that God is faithful to do what He has promised, and that He not only desires good things for us, but that He is also utterly trustworthy to give us the answers that we need. From there, we go to other topical listings of verses that can be used to pray about particular subjects, such as healing, the need for provision, and salvation for loved ones.

As you read through these verses frequently and meditate on them, your faith will increase. You may wish to read them aloud, because *"faith comes by **hearing**, and hearing by the word of God"* (Romans 10:17). In addition, you will find it helpful to have verses that apply to a particular need listed together, so that you have them at your fingertips when you need to effectively press your case before the Lord's throne. He loves it when we use His Word like that!

May you obtain your prayer answers as you skillfully wield the Word of God, and may this book be a blessing-tool to help you achieve that goal.

~ *Lee Ann*

A Place to Begin

Your Importance as an Intercessor

We need to realize that our call to intercession is very important in the Lord's eyes. People tend to minimize the importance of prayer, but God does not. God loves the heart of the intercessor.

Two Persons of the Godhead, the Holy Spirit and Jesus, are actively and continuously interceding. Romans 8:26 tells us that *"the Spirit himself makes intercession for us with groanings which cannot be uttered,"* while Romans 8:34 goes on to say that *"Christ who died, yes rather, who is risen again, who is even at the right hand of God, ... also makes intercession for us."* In intercession, we are partnering with Jesus and the Holy Spirit in praying for what is already on Father's heart -- IF we pray according to the revealed will of God in Scripture, coupled with staying sensitive to the Spirit's prompting and leading.

Whether you feel valuable as an intercessor or not, you are. Whether you feel your prayers are important or not, they are. But please do not take just my word for it. Let's see what the Bible says:

I have set watchmen upon your walls, O Jerusalem, which shall never hold their peace day or night. You who make mention of the LORD, do not keep silence, and give him no rest, until he establishes, and until he makes Jerusalem a praise in the earth.
-- Isaiah 62:6, 7

And I sought for a man among them that would make up the hedge and stand in the gap before me for the land, so that I would not destroy it: but I found none.
-- Ezekiel 22:30

And he saw that there was no man and wondered that there was no intercessor: therefore his arm brought salvation to him, and his own righteousness sustained him.
-- Isaiah 59:16

If any man sees his brother sin a sin which is not unto death, he shall ask, and he [God] shall give him life for those who do not sin unto death ….
-- 1 John 5:16

And the prayer of faith shall save the sick, and the Lord shall raise him up: and if he has committed sins, they shall be forgiven him. … Pray for one another, so that you may be healed. The effective fervent prayer of a righteous man avails much.
-- James 5:15, 16

However, this kind [of demon] will not go out except by prayer and fasting.
-- Matthew 17:21

There are countless examples of people in the Bible who took intercession seriously and got answers. Abraham, Job, Moses, Aaron, King Hezekiah, and many of the Old Testament prophets were intercessors. The Apostle Paul was as well. The following references tell a few of their stories. I encourage you to read them, so that you can see what God can do through your prayers:

Abraham: Genesis 18:16-33 and Genesis 20:17, 18

Job: Job 42:7-10
Moses: Exodus 32:9-14
Moses and Aaron: Numbers 16:43-50
King Hezekiah: 2 Chronicles 30:18-20
Amos: Amos 7:1-6
Daniel: Daniel 9:1-19 (brought about the return of Israel to their land)

Never, ever, question the significance of your ministry as an intercessor. The intercession of God's people is a primary tool that He uses to advance His Kingdom in the earth today.

Establishing Our Foundations for Prayer

The Bible Is True

If we are to go anywhere in prayer in more than a hit-and-miss fashion, we must have it firmly established in our hearts and minds that God's Word is true. This means all of it. Because His Word is unshakably true, we can count on it to bring forth the results we need it to produce when we apply portions of it to our intercessions.

Isaiah 55:10, 11 declares, *"For as the rain and the snow come down from heaven and do not return there, but water the earth and make it bring forth and bud, that it may give seed to the sower and bread to the eater, so shall my word be that goes forth from my mouth. It shall not return to me void, but it shall accomplish that which I please, and it shall prosper in the thing whereto I sent it."*

When we pray the Word, we can know that it will bring forth results. We can trust its reliability to be rock-solid.

This is what God says about the truthfulness of His Word:

The law of the LORD is perfect, converting the soul: the testimony of the LORD is sure, making the simple wise.
-- Psalm 19:7

As for God, his way is perfect; the word of the LORD is tried. He is a buckler to all those who trust in him.
-- Psalm 18:30

Sanctify them through your truth: your word is truth.
-- John 17:17

… The Scripture cannot be broken.
-- John 10:35

The words of the LORD are pure words: as silver tried in a furnace of earth, purified seven times.
-- Psalm 12:6

Your word is very pure: therefore your servant loves it.

Your righteousness is an everlasting righteousness, and your law is the truth.
-- Psalm 119:140, 142

Your testimonies are very sure: holiness becomes your house, O LORD, forever.
-- Psalm 93:5

Your word is true from the beginning, and every one of your righteous judgments endures forever.
-- Psalm 119:160

Every word of God is pure: he is a shield to them who put their trust in him.
-- Proverbs 30:5

And now, O Lord GOD, you are that God, and your words are true, and you have promised this goodness to your servant.
-- 2 Samuel 7:28

Into your hand I commit my spirit: you have redeemed me, O LORD God of truth.
-- Psalm 31:5

For the word of the LORD is right, and all his works are done in truth.
-- Psalm 33:4

For the LORD is good; his mercy is everlasting, and his truth endures to all generations.
-- Psalm 100:5

...Which God, who cannot lie, promised before the world began.
-- Titus 1:2

That by two immutable [absolutely unchangeable] things, in which it is impossible for God to lie, we might have a strong consolation, who have fled for refuge to lay hold upon the hope set before us.
-- Hebrews 6:18

God Intends for Us to Know His Will

Many traditions that the Church has accepted over the years are not good Bible truth. In some circles, people have been taught that we cannot know the specific will of God for our lives or for certain situations. This is not true, as we will see in the Word.

If we are to be effective in receiving answers to prayer, the best way to pray is from a place of understanding what God's will is in a particular set of circumstances. We may not have the full counsel of the Lord, but as we pray about what we do know to be His will, He can show us more details.

1 John 5:14, 15 tells us, *"And this is the confidence that we have in him, that, if we ask anything **according to his will**, he hears us -- and if we know that he hears us, whatever we ask, we know that we have the petitions that we desired of him."* You can see by this verse that knowing His will and praying according to it brings answers.

Here are some verses that assure us we can know God's will:

He will guide the meek in judgment, and he will teach the meek his way.

What man is he who fears the LORD? He shall teach him in the way that he shall choose.

The secret of the LORD is with them who fear him; and he will show them his covenant.

My eyes are ever toward the LORD, for he shall pluck my feet out of the net.

-- Psalm 25:9, 12, 14, 15

Wherefore, do not be unwise, but understanding what the will of the Lord is.
    -- Ephesians 5:17

Cause me to know the way wherein I should walk.
    -- Psalm 143:8

And your ears shall hear a word behind you, saying, "This is the way: walk in it," when you turn to the right hand, and when you turn to the left.
    -- Isaiah 30:21

I will instruct you and teach you in the way in which you shall go; I will guide you with my eye.
    -- Psalm 32:8

Surely the LORD GOD will do nothing without first revealing his secret to his servants the prophets.
    -- Amos 3:7

The way of the slothful man is as a hedge of thorns, but the way of the righteous is made plain.
    -- Proverbs 15:19

For you will light my candle; the LORD my God will enlighten my darkness.
    -- Psalm 18:2

For this cause we also, since the day we heard it, do not cease to pray for you and to desire that you might be filled with the knowledge of his will in all wisdom and spiritual understanding.
    -- Colossians 1:9

And I will bring the blind by a way that they did not know; I will lead them in paths that they have not known. I will make darkness light before them and crooked things straight. These things will I do for them, and I will not forsake them.

    -- Isaiah 42:16

I have not spoken in secret, in a dark place of the earth. I did not say to the seed of Jacob, "Seek me in vain." I the LORD speak righteousness; I declare things that are right.

    -- Isaiah 45:19

For the upright, light arises in the darkness ….

    -- Psalm 112:4

I have taught you in the way of wisdom; I have led you in right paths. When you go, your steps shall not be straitened, and when you run, you shall not stumble.

    -- Proverbs 4:11, 12

Consider what I say, and the Lord give you understanding in all things.

    -- 2 Timothy 2:7

The entrance of your words gives light; it gives understanding to the simple.

    -- Psalm 119:130

God Promises to Guide His Children

Sometimes we get panicky because we have decisions to make and don't quite know what to do. Or, perhaps we have a desperate need to pray about, but we feel helpless and overwhelmed about where to begin, how to tackle it. God has promised in His Word to guide us, whether it is in making a decision, knowing how to pray, or in the overall picture of where our lives are supposed to go. The key is simply to ask Him to guide us, and then rest in believing faith that He will do as we have asked.

When you are feeling a little uncertain, or even very shaky, about what's next, these verses will help you to have confidence that His eye is upon you and that He will lead the way:

But made his own people to go forth like sheep and guided them in the wilderness like a flock. And he led them on safely, so that they did not fear.
  -- Psalm 78:52, 53

I will hear what God the LORD will speak: for he will speak peace to his people and to his saints: but let them not turn again to folly.
Righteousness shall go before him and shall set us in the way of his steps.
  -- Psalm 85:8, 13

Teach me your way, O LORD; I will walk in your truth. Unite my heart to fear your name.
  -- Psalm 86:11

Cause me to hear your loving-kindness in the morning, for it is in you that I trust. Cause me to know the way in which I should walk, for I lift up my soul to you.

Teach me to do your will, for you are my God. Your Spirit is good; lead me into the land of uprightness.
    -- Psalm 143:8, 10

And the LORD shall guide you continually, and satisfy your soul in drought, and make your bones fat: and you shall be like a watered garden, and like a spring of water, whose waters do not fail.
    -- Isaiah 58:11

For his God instructs him to discretion and teaches him.
    -- Isaiah 28:26

This is what the LORD says, your Redeemer, the Holy One of Israel: "I am the LORD your God who teaches you to profit, who leads you by the way that you should go."
    -- Isaiah 48:17

… Therefore for your name's sake lead me and guide me.
    -- Psalm 31:3

I will bless the LORD, who has given me counsel; my reins [thoughts of the heart] also instruct me in the night seasons.
    -- Psalm 16:7

The steps of a good man are ordered by the LORD, and he delights in his way.
    -- Psalm 37:23

But the path of the just is as the shining light, that shines more and more unto the perfect day.

    -- Proverbs 4:18

For this God is our God forever and ever: he will be our guide even unto death.

    -- Psalm 48:14

Nevertheless, I am continually with you; you have held me by my right hand. You shall guide me with your counsel and afterward receive me to glory.

    -- Psalm 73:23, 24

Commit your works to the LORD, and your thoughts shall be established.

    -- Proverbs 16:3

And he led them forth by the right way ....

    -- Psalm 107:7

In all your ways acknowledge him, and he shall direct your paths.

    -- Proverbs 3:6

God's Promises Shall Stand

We already established in our second chapter, *The Bible Is True*, that the Word of God is completely trustworthy. Every promise in it is immovable as a mountain. We can carry this a step further to assert that every personal promise which He gives us shall also stand firm.

We must be careful with this idea, because although the Bible promises to all believers are infallible, when it comes to personal promises we receive from God, we can make mistakes in our hearing or our interpretation of what He has said. But when we hear a promise from the Lord and He continues to speak about it over a period of time, when it lines up with Scripture and godly counsel from wise people, and when it is confirmed through other means, we can know that no matter what the circumstances may look like along the way, God will surely perform for us what He has said.

When the way before you looks bleak, and your promises seem dim, encourage yourself with these verses:

Not one iota failed of any good thing which the LORD had spoken to the house of Israel.
-- Joshua 21:45

… And you know in all your hearts and in all your souls, that not one thing has failed of all the good things which the LORD your God spoke concerning you. All have come to pass for you, and not one thing has failed thereof.
-- Joshua 23:14

God is not a man, that he should lie; neither the son of man, that he should repent [change his mind]. Has he said, and shall he not do it? Or has he spoken, and shall he not make it good?

    -- Numbers 23:19

Declaring the end from the beginning, and from ancient times the things that are not yet done, saying, "My counsel shall stand, and I will do all my pleasure. ...Yes, I have spoken it, and I will also bring it to pass; I have purposed it, and I will also do it."

    -- Isaiah 46:10, 11

And blessed is she who believed: for there shall be a performance of those things which were told her from the Lord.

    -- Luke 1:45

Forever, O LORD, your word is settled in heaven.

    -- Psalm 119:89

For as the rain and the snow come down from heaven and do not return there, but water the earth, and make it bring forth and bud, that it may give seed to the sower and bread to the eater, so shall my word be that goes forth from my mouth. It shall not return to me void, but it shall accomplish that which I please, and it shall prosper in the thing for which I sent it.

    -- Isaiah 55:10, 11

Nevertheless, my loving-kindness will I not utterly take from him, nor suffer my faithfulness to fail. I will not break My covenant, nor alter the thing that is gone out of my lips.

    -- Psalm 89:33, 34

… For I have pronounced the word, says the LORD.
-- Jeremiah 34:5

The grass withers, the flower fades, but the word of our God shall stand forever.
-- Isaiah 40:8

And this shall be a sign to you from the LORD, that the LORD will do this thing that he has spoken.
What shall I say? He has both spoken to me, and he himself has done it ….
-- Isaiah 38:7, 15

For he spoke, and it was done; he commanded, and it stood fast. The LORD brings the counsel of the heathen to nothing; he makes the devices of the people of no effect. The counsel of the LORD stands forever; the thoughts of his heart to all generations.
-- Psalm 33:9-11

And, behold, I am with you and will keep you in all places wherever you go, and I will bring you again into this land: for I will not leave you until I have done that which I have spoken to you about.
-- Genesis 28:15

I have declared the former things from the beginning, and they went forth out of my mouth, and I showed them; I did them suddenly, and they came to pass.
-- Isaiah 48:3

For all the promises of God in him are yes, and in him Amen, to the glory of God by us.
-- 2 Corinthians 1:20

For surely there is an end, and your expectation shall not be cut off.
-- Proverbs 23:18

… For you have magnified your word above all your name.
-- Psalm 138:2

The LORD of hosts has sworn, saying, "Surely as I have thought, so it shall come to pass; and as I have purposed, so it shall stand."
For the LORD of hosts has purposed, and who shall disannul it? And his hand is stretched out, and who shall turn it back?
-- Isaiah 14:24, 27

For I am the LORD: I will speak, and the word that I speak shall come to pass ....
-- Ezekiel 12:25

He has remembered his covenant forever, the word he commanded to a thousand generations.
-- Psalm 105:8

Who has kept with your servant David my father that which you promised him; you spoke also with your mouth, and have fulfilled it with your hand, as it is this day.
-- I Kings 8:24

Who confirms the word of his servant and performs the counsel of his messengers ....
-- Isaiah 44:26

… For I watch over my word to perform it.
-- Jeremiah 1:12 (ASV)

He [Abraham] did not stagger at the promise of God through unbelief, but was strong in faith, giving glory to God, being fully persuaded that what he had promised he was able also to perform.

    -- Romans 4:20, 21

God Means Great Good Toward Us

I find that one of the biggest obstacles many of us must overcome in our journey with the Lord is not fully believing in His goodness toward us. We want to believe, but, perhaps because of our fallen, sinful nature, or perhaps due to hurts and disappointments we have received from other people, we tend to struggle with absolutely trusting God to be consistently good to us.

We must change our untrusting mindset, and one of the best ways to do that is by frequently meditating on the Bible verses which assure us of His goodness. When we get the goodness factor straightened out in our thinking, doubt and mistrust have nowhere to hide, and faith can soar.

Here are some verses to help you understand God's good intentions toward you:

And we know that all things work together for good to those who love God, to those who are the called according to his purpose.
-- Romans 8:28

For I know the thoughts that I think toward you, says the LORD, thoughts of peace, and not of evil, to give you an expected end.
-- Jeremiah 29:11

For I know the plans I have for you, declares the LORD, plans to prosper you and not to harm you, plans to give you hope and a future.
-- Jeremiah 29:11 (NIV)

For the LORD God is a sun and shield; the LORD will give grace and glory. No good thing will he withhold from those who walk uprightly.

-- Psalm 84:11

O fear the LORD, his saints, for there is no want to those who fear him. The young lions lack and suffer hunger, but they who seek the LORD shall not want any good thing.

-- Psalm 34:9, 10

Yes, the LORD shall give that which is good, and our land shall yield her increase.

-- Psalm 85:12

The thief only comes to steal, and to kill, and to destroy: I have come so that they might have life and that they might have it more abundantly.

-- John 10:10

Every good gift and every perfect gift is from above, and comes down from the Father of lights, with whom is no variableness, neither shadow of turning.

-- James 1:17

Blessed is the Lord, who daily loads us with benefits, even the God of our salvation.

-- Psalm 68:19

Oh how great is your goodness which you have laid up for those who fear you, which you have wrought for those who trust in you before the sons of men!

-- Psalm 31:19

What man is there among you, whom, if his son asks for bread, he will give him a stone? Or, if he asks for a fish, will he give him a serpent? If you then, being evil, know how to give good gifts to your children, how much more shall your Father who is in heaven give good things to those who ask him?
    -- Matthew 7:9-11

Bless the LORD, O my soul, and do not forget all his benefits: who forgives all your iniquities, who heals all your diseases, who redeems your life from destruction, who crowns you with loving-kindness and tender mercies, who satisfies your mouth with good things, so that your youth is renewed like the eagle's.
    -- Psalm 103:2-5

For I will set my eyes upon them for good, and I will bring them again to this land. I will build them and not pull them down, and I will plant them and not pluck them up. And I will give them a heart to know me, that I am the LORD. And they shall be my people, and I will be their God, for they shall return to me with their whole heart.
    -- Jeremiah 24:6, 7

The LORD is gracious and full of compassion, slow to anger and of great mercy. The LORD is good to all, and his tender mercies are over all his works.
    -- Psalm 145:8, 9

Bring my soul out of prison, so that I may praise your name. The righteous shall encompass me roundabout, for you shall deal bountifully with me.
    -- Psalm 142:7

But my God shall supply all your need according to his riches in glory by Christ Jesus.
    -- Philippians 4:19

The LORD takes my part with those who help me ….
    -- Psalm 118:7

When I cry unto you, then shall my enemies turn back: this I know, for God is for me.
    -- Psalm 56:9

What shall we then say to these things? If God is for us, who can be against us? He who did not spare his own Son, but delivered him up for us all, how shall he not with him also freely give us all things?
    -- Romans 8:31, 32

For he satisfies the longing soul and fills the hungry soul with goodness.
    -- Psalm 107:9

Though a sinner does evil a hundred times, and his days are prolonged, yet surely I know that it shall be well with them who fear God, who fear before him.
    -- Ecclesiastes 8:12

For the mountains shall depart and the hills be removed, but my kindness shall not depart from you, neither shall the covenant of my peace be removed, says the LORD who has mercy on you.
    -- Isaiah 54:10

God Will Not Let Us Be Ashamed When We Have Hoped in Him

Some of you have questions about things you have held dear and have invested much prayer into:

- *What if God doesn't come through for me on this after all?*
- *What if He **can't** answer because people throw a wrench in the works?*
- *What if I didn't hear Him right in the first place and I'm praying in a wrong direction?*
- *What if I end up looking like a fool for believing so hard for my answer?*

Whenever we believe God for big things, it will look risky. But when you believe God for His best and go after Him with all your heart, humbly submitting yourself to His will, it's going to turn out all right.

You will make a few mistakes in the journey of learning to be a mature intercessor. There may be a few things you won't get exactly right in your understanding of how to pray. But He will correct your course and nudge you in the right direction as you continue to seek Him on any particular prayer matter.

And He will not let you be ashamed. God is not in the business of leaving you to your own devices or stranding you high and dry. He's going to answer, and you're going to come out of whatever prayer concern you face with His grace and favor covering you.

Here are some verses to help you rest and not be afraid of shame:

O my God, I trust in you: do not let me be ashamed; do not let my enemies triumph over me. Yes, let no one who waits on you be ashamed. Instead, let them be ashamed who transgress without cause.
     -- Psalm 25:2, 3

... Behold, I lay in Zion a chief cornerstone -- elect, precious. And he who believes on him shall not be confounded.
     -- I Peter 2:6

In you, O LORD, I put my trust: let me never be ashamed. Deliver me in your righteousness.

But I trusted in you, O LORD. I said, "You are my God."

Do not let me be ashamed, O LORD, for I have called upon you ….
     -- Psalm 31:1, 14, 17

The LORD redeems the soul of his servants, and not one of them who trust in him shall be desolate.
     -- Psalm 34:22

In you, O LORD, I put my trust: let me never be put to confusion.
     -- Psalm 71:1

Uphold me according to your word, that I may live -- and do not let me be ashamed of my hope.
     -- Psalm 119:116

Our fathers trusted in you; they trusted, and you delivered them. They cried unto you and were delivered; they trusted in you and were not confounded.
     -- Psalm 22:4, 5

They looked unto him and were lightened, and their faces were not ashamed.
-- Psalm 34:5

For the Scripture says, "Whoever believes on him shall not be ashamed."
-- Romans 10:11

… And you shall know that I am the LORD: for they shall not be ashamed who wait for me.
-- Isaiah 49:23

For the Lord GOD will help me; therefore I shall not be confounded. Therefore I have set my face like a flint, and I know that I shall not be ashamed.
-- Isaiah 50:7

… We glory in tribulations also, knowing that tribulations work patience; and patience, experience; and experience, hope. And hope does not make us ashamed, because the love of God is shed abroad in our hearts by the Holy Spirit who is given to us.
-- Romans 5:3-5

I wait for the LORD; my soul waits, and in his word do I hope.
-- Psalm 130:5

Blessed is the man who trusts in the LORD and whose hope is in the LORD. For he shall be as a tree planted by the waters, that spreads out her roots by the river, and shall not see when heat comes, but her leaf shall be green. She shall not be careful in the year of drought, neither shall cease from yielding fruit.
-- Jeremiah 17:7, 8

The hope of the righteous shall be gladness, but the expectation of the wicked shall perish.
-- Proverbs 10:28

… I have trusted also in the LORD; therefore I shall not slide.
-- Psalm 26:1

Fear not, for you shall not be ashamed; neither be confounded, for you shall not be put to shame. For you shall forget the shame of your youth and shall not remember the reproach of your widowhood anymore.
-- Isaiah 54:4

Our soul waits for the LORD: he is our help and our shield. For our heart shall rejoice in him, because we have trusted in his holy name. Let your mercy, O LORD, be upon us, accordingly as we hope in you.
-- Psalm 33:20-22

Cast your burden upon the LORD, and he shall sustain you. He shall never suffer the righteous to be moved.
-- Psalm 55:22

And you shall eat in plenty and be satisfied, and praise the name of the LORD your God, who has dealt wondrously with you: and my people shall never be ashamed. And you shall know that I am in the midst of Israel, and that I am the LORD your God, and there is no other: and my people shall never be ashamed.
-- Joel 2:26, 27

I have stuck to your testimonies. O LORD, do not put me to shame.
-- Psalm 119:31

God Helps Those Who Trust in Him

Trusting in God during stormy or uncertain times is a challenge we all face. None of us will manage to live through a lifetime without having crises confront us which test our faith. God uses these crises to wreck our independence. You see, our flesh wants to have control. We want to be the ones calling the shots and fixing our own circumstances. Adam and Eve fell because of a desire for independence. God wants us to be dependent upon Him, just as Adam and Eve were dependent in their perfect state. Through dependence, He works intimate relationship between us and Him. It is a restoring of what was lost in Eden.

In the midst of our stresses, God understands how shaky it feels for us -- and He wants us to know that He will most certainly come to our aid if we will only put our hand in His. Trust is not easy. For some of us, it is harder than for others.

The following verses were spoken by the Lord to assure us that He will help us as we depend on Him:

Blessed is that man who makes the LORD his trust ....
    -- Psalm 40:4

The LORD is good, a stronghold in the day of trouble: and he knows those who trust in him.
    -- Nahum 1:7

But let all those who put their trust in you rejoice; let them ever shout for joy, because you defend them. Let them also who love your name be joyful in you.
    -- Psalm 5:11

And they who know your name will put their trust in you: for you, LORD, have not forsaken those who seek you.
-- Psalm 9:10

And the LORD shall help them and deliver them. He shall deliver them from the wicked and save them, because they trust in him.
-- Psalm 37:40

The LORD redeems the soul of his servants, and not one of them who trust in him shall be desolate.
-- Psalm 34:22

Show your marvelous loving-kindness, O you who save by your right hand them who put their trust in you from those that rise up against them.
-- Psalm 17:7

The LORD is my strength and my shield; my heart trusted in him, and I am helped ....
-- Psalm 28:7

Many sorrows shall be to the wicked, but he who trusts in the LORD, mercy shall encompass him round about.
-- Psalm 32:10

... I have trusted also in the LORD; therefore I shall not slide.
-- Psalm 26:1

... For they cried to God in the battle, and he was entreated of them because they put their trust in him.
-- I Chronicles 5:20

... Whoever puts his trust in the LORD shall be safe.
-- Proverbs 29:25

God's Faithfulness Is Unfailing

Faithfulness is the very fabric of which integrity is made. We've all been betrayed or let down by people to one degree or another. But God, because of His very nature, is incapable of failing in His faithfulness toward us. His faithfulness is the basis for the trust we place in Him, and it can be rested upon.

And I saw heaven opened, and behold, a white horse, and he who sat upon him was called Faithful and True ....
    -- Revelation 19:11

For I have said, "Mercy shall be built up forever. You shall establish your faithfulness in the very heavens."
    -- Psalm 89:2

Nevertheless, my loving-kindness I will not utterly take from him, nor suffer my faithfulness to fail.
    -- Psalm 89:33

If we do not believe, yet he abides faithful: he cannot deny himself.
    -- 2 Timothy 2:13

Let us hold fast the profession of our faith without wavering, for he is faithful who promised.
    -- Hebrews 10:23

Your mercy, O LORD, is in the heavens, and your faithfulness reaches to the clouds.
    -- Psalm 36:5

Your faithfulness is to all generations; you have established the earth, and it abides.
  -- Psalm 119:90

But the Lord is faithful, who shall establish you and keep you from evil.
  -- 2 Thessalonians 3:3

Jesus Christ the same yesterday, and today, and forever.
  -- Hebrews 13:8

Faithful is he who calls you, who also will do it.
  -- 1 Thessalonians 5:24

… I will not fail you, nor forsake you.
  -- Joshua 1:5

Your testimonies that you have commanded are righteous and very faithful.
  -- Psalm 119:138

Know therefore that the LORD your God, he is God, the faithful God, who keeps covenant and mercy with those who love him and keep his commandments to a thousand generations.
  -- Deuteronomy 7:9

… But God is faithful, who will not suffer you to be tempted above what you are able [to handle], but will with the temptation also make a way to escape, so that you may be able to bear it.
  -- 1 Corinthians 10:13

For the mountains shall depart and the hills be removed, but my kindness shall not depart from you, neither shall the covenant of my peace be removed, says the LORD who has mercy on you.

-- Isaiah 54:10

He has remembered his covenant forever, the word he commanded to a thousand generations.

-- Psalm 105:8

God Has Not Forgotten You

In seasons of discouragement, or when life doesn't seem to be moving forward for us as fast as it should, it is common to feel like we have disappeared from God's radar screen. All the time, God is steadily working on our behalf, but when we can't see it with our eyes, our faith must do the seeing for us.

We can help our faith-sight do what it needs to do by agreeing with what God says about His remembrance of us, and these verses will assist you:

He has given meat [food] to them who fear him: he will ever be mindful of his covenant.
> -- Psalm 111:5

Surely he [the righteous man who fears the Lord] shall not be moved forever. The righteous shall be in everlasting remembrance.
> -- Psalm 112:6

But Zion said, "The LORD has forsaken me, and my Lord has forgotten me." Can a woman forget her nursing child, that she would not have compassion on the son of her womb? Yes, they may forget, yet I will not forget you. Behold, I have engraved you upon the palms of my hands; your walls are continually before me.
> -- Isaiah 49:14-16

For the LORD will not cast off his people; neither will he forsake his inheritance.
> -- Psalm 94:14

Are not five sparrows sold for two farthings, and not one of them is forgotten before God? But even the very hairs of your head are all numbered. Fear not, therefore: you are of more value than many sparrows.
        -- Luke 12:6, 7

... I will not fail you, nor forsake you.
        -- Joshua 1:5

... For I will not leave you until I have done that which I have spoken to you of.
        -- Genesis 28:15

... For he has said, "I will never leave you, nor forsake you."
        -- Hebrews 13:5

When he makes inquisition for blood, he remembers them; he does not forget the cry of the humble.
        -- Psalm 9:12

For God is not unrighteous to forget your work and labor of love, which you have showed toward his name ....
        -- Hebrews 6:10

When my father and my mother forsake me, then the LORD will take me up.
        -- Psalm 27:10

For the LORD loves judgment and does not forsake his saints; they are preserved forever. But the seed of the wicked shall be cut off.
        -- Psalm 37:28

For he has not despised nor abhorred the affliction of the afflicted; neither has he hidden his face from him; but when he cried to him, he heard.
-- Psalm 22:24

When the poor and needy seek water, and there is none, and their tongues fail for thirst, I the LORD will hear them. I the God of Israel will not forsake them.
-- Isaiah 41:17

And I will strengthen the house of Judah, and I will save the house of Joseph, and I will bring them again to place them. For I have mercy upon them, and they shall be as though I had not cast them off: for I am the LORD their God, and will hear them.
-- Zechariah 10:6

For I said in my haste, "I am cut off from before your eyes." Nevertheless, you heard the voice of my supplications when I cried to you.
-- Psalm 31:22

We Need Not Fear

"Fear not." Seventy-four times the Bible uses this phrase. Fear is a powerful adversary and a major hindrance to effective prayer. It keeps us focused on how big the problems are, so that we cannot concentrate on praying through to victory over them.

Fear is an enemy that we all face. The man who says he is never tempted to fear is either in denial or lying. But we do not have to throw up our hands in defeat; we do not have to bow the knee to fear. Jesus intends for us to overcome it -- and He will be right by our side, helping us to do it.

What is our part in overcoming fear? We must repent of having indulged it, renounce its hold on our lives, and resist it. We must also recognize that resisting fear will be an ongoing challenge. Knowing what God has to say about fear and using His Word as a weapon of our spiritual warfare to overcome it are essential.

These verses will help you win your battle against fear:

For God has not given us the spirit of fear, but of power, and of love, and of a sound mind.
-- 2 Timothy 1:7

There is no fear in love; instead, perfect love casts out fear, because fear has torment.
-- 1 John 4:18

41

Fear not, for I am with you; do not be dismayed, for I am your God. I will strengthen you -- yes, I will help you. Yes, I will uphold you with the right hand of my righteousness.
    -- Isaiah 41:10

... Fear not; stand still, and see the salvation of the LORD, which he will show to you today: for the Egyptians whom you have seen today, you shall see them again no more forever. The LORD shall fight for you, and you shall hold your peace.
    -- Exodus 14:13, 14

Fear not, little flock, for it is your Father's good pleasure to give you the kingdom.
    -- Luke 12:32

Aren't five sparrows sold for two farthings, and not one of them is forgotten before God? But even the very hairs of your head are all numbered. Fear not, therefore: you are of more value than many sparrows.
    -- Luke 12:6, 7

... Fear not, for I have redeemed you. I have called you by your name; you are mine. When you pass through the waters, I will be with you, and through the rivers, they shall not overflow you. When you walk through the fire, you shall not be burned; neither shall the flame kindle upon you.
    -- Isaiah 43:1, 2

You will keep in perfect peace the one whose mind is stayed on you, because he trusts in you.
    -- Isaiah 26:3

And let the peace of God rule in your hearts ....
    -- Colossians 3:15

For I the LORD your God will hold your right hand, saying to you, "Fear not; I will help you."
-- Isaiah 41:13

Say to those who are of a fearful heart, "Be strong, fear not. Behold, your God will come with vengeance, even God with a recompense. He will come and save you."
-- Isaiah 35:4

He shall not be afraid of evil tidings; his heart is fixed, trusting in the LORD. His heart is established; he shall not be afraid, until he sees his desire upon his enemies.
-- Psalm 112:7, 8

Do not be afraid of sudden fear, neither of the desolation of the wicked when it comes. For the LORD shall be your confidence and shall keep your foot from being taken.
-- Proverbs 3:25, 26

Fear not, for you shall not be ashamed. Neither be confounded, for you shall not be put to shame: for you shall forget the shame of your youth, and shall not remember the reproach of your widowhood anymore.
-- Isaiah 54:4

And it is the LORD who goes before you. He will be with you; he will not fail you, neither forsake you. Fear not, neither be dismayed.
-- Deuteronomy 31:8

Have I not commanded you? Be strong and of a good courage; do not be afraid, neither be dismayed: for the LORD your God is with you wherever you go.
-- Joshua 1:9

The LORD is on my side; I will not fear. What can man do to me?

-- Psalm 118:6

You shall not be afraid for the terror by night, nor for the arrow that flies by day, nor for the pestilence that walks in darkness, nor for the destruction that wastes at noonday. A thousand shall fall at your side and ten thousand at your right hand, but it shall not come near you.

-- Psalm 91:5-7

I, even I, am he who comforts you. Who are you, that you should be afraid of a man that shall die, and of the son of man who shall be made as grass; and forget the LORD your Maker, who has stretched forth the heavens, and laid the foundations of the earth; and you have feared continually every day because of the fury of the oppressor, as if he were ready to destroy? And where is the fury of the oppressor?

-- Isaiah 51:12, 13

Our God Is Our Safety

If we intercede from a position of fear in any particular situation, we will often end up praying amiss. That is one of the reasons why we laid the foundation in the last chapter that we must overcome fear in order to pray effectively.

God does not only give us the commandment not to fear, however, and then leave us to deal with fear-generating circumstances on our own. He takes it a step further to assure us that in Him we will always be safe. *He* is watching out for us.

The following Scriptures are further encouragement not to fear -- because God is fully trustworthy to keep us, and those whom we pray for, from harm:

The horse is prepared against the day of battle, but safety is of the LORD.
-- Proverbs 21:31

The eternal God is your refuge, and underneath are the everlasting arms ....
-- Deuteronomy 33:27

For the oppression of the poor, for the sighing of the needy, now I will arise, says the LORD; I will set him in safety from him who puffs at him.
-- Psalm 12:5

Be merciful to me, O God, be merciful to me, for my soul trusts in you. Yes, in the shadow of your wings I will make my refuge until these calamities are a thing of the past.
-- Psalm 57:1

The name of the LORD is a strong tower; the righteous man runs into it and is safe.
-- Proverbs 18:10

The fear of man brings a snare, but whoever puts his trust in the LORD shall be safe.
-- Proverbs 29:25

For in the time of trouble he shall hide me in his pavilion. In the secret of his tabernacle shall he hide me; he shall set me up upon a rock.
-- Psalm 27:5

You shall hide them [who fear you] in the secret of your presence from the pride of man; you shall keep them secretly in a pavilion from the strife of tongues.
-- Psalm 31:20

Deliver me, O LORD, from my enemies; I flee unto you to hide me.
-- Psalm 143:9

Trust in him at all times; you people, pour out your heart before him. God is a refuge for us.
-- Psalm 62:8

I will both lie down in peace and sleep, for you, LORD, make me dwell only in safety.
-- Psalm 4:8

And you shall be secure, because there is hope; yes, you shall dig around you, and you shall take your rest in safety. Also, you shall lie down, and no one shall make you afraid; yes, many shall court you.
    -- Job 11:18, 19

Hold me up and I shall be safe, and I will have respect unto your statutes continually.
    -- Psalm 119:117

Be my strong habitation whereunto I may continually resort. You have given commandment to save me, for you are my rock and my fortress.
    -- Psalm 71:3

You save me from violence.

You have delivered me from the violent man.
    -- 2 Samuel 22:3, 49

And he led them on safely, so that they did not fear, but the sea overwhelmed their enemies.
    -- Psalm 78:53

For you shall not go out with haste, nor go by flight: for the LORD will go before you, and the God of Israel will be your rearward.
    -- Isaiah 52:12

We know that whoever is born of God does not sin: but he who is begotten of God keeps him, and that wicked one does not touch him.
    -- I John 5:18

All of Psalm 91

You Can Have Peace

Peace is part of our inheritance in Christ. It is mentioned as a fruit of the Spirit in Galatians 5:22, which means it is a characteristic that we can increase in. Peace is also something we can choose to dwell in. In other words, when the temptation to wring our hands comes knocking, we can resist it, mentally put our hand in Jesus' hand, and declare, "Lord, I am determining to trust You and not let myself get ruffled."

Strengthen your ability to dwell in peace by meditating on these verses:

Therefore being justified by faith, we have peace with God through our Lord Jesus Christ.
   -- Romans 5:1

You will keep in perfect peace the one whose mind is stayed on you, because he trusts in you.
   -- Isaiah 26:3

Do not be care-filled for anything, but in everything by prayer and supplication with thanksgiving let your requests be made known to God. And the peace of God, which passes all understanding, shall keep your hearts and minds through Christ Jesus.
   -- Philippians 4:6, 7

Peace I leave with you; my peace I give to you: not as the world gives, give I to you. Do not let your heart be troubled; neither let it be afraid.
   -- John 14:27

These things I have spoken to you, that in me you might have peace. In the world you shall have tribulation, but be of good cheer: I have overcome the world.
-- John 16:33

I will both lie down in peace, and sleep: for you, LORD, make me dwell only in safety.
-- Psalm 4:8

The LORD will give strength to his people; the LORD will bless his people with peace.
-- Psalm 29:11

They who love your law have great peace, and nothing shall offend them.
-- Psalm 119:165

And let the peace of God rule in your hearts, to which you are also called in one body, and be thankful.
-- Colossians 3:15

For the kingdom of God is not meat [food] and drink, but righteousness, and peace, and joy in the Holy Ghost.
-- Romans 14:17

And the work of righteousness shall be peace, and the effect of righteousness, quiet and assurance forever.
-- Isaiah 32:17

Our God Is a Listening God

God intently listens to the cries of His children. We can be certain that when we pray, He is eager to hear *and answer*. Unfortunately, some of us have been taught that prayer petitions are not meant to bring answers; they are only meant to make us feel better. Frankly, I don't find much "feel better" in having little hope of God answering!

Scripture firmly establishes that God not only hears, but when He hears, He answers. In this chapter and the next, you will find Bible verses that assure us of His listening ear and His answering hand. I would like to clarify that although the verses in this chapter speak of God hearing, they are not just telling us that He is compassionately listening. "Hearing," in the Bible, has the understanding attached to it that an audience with the King is in session, that He is carefully considering the petition, and that He is intending to grant it.

Therefore I will look to the LORD; I will wait for the God of my salvation. My God will hear me.
  -- Micah 7:7

For the eyes of the Lord are over the righteous, and his ears are open to their prayers ....
  -- I Peter 3:12

If I regard iniquity [wickedness] in my heart, the Lord will not hear me. But of a surety God has heard me; he has attended to the voice of my prayer. Blessed be God who has not turned away my prayer nor his mercy from me.
  -- Psalm 66:18-20

O thou that hearest prayer, unto thee shall all flesh come.
-- Psalm 65:2 (KJV)

For the LORD hears the poor and does not despise his prisoners.
-- Psalm 69:33

Give ear, O LORD, to my prayer, and attend to the voice of my supplications. In the day of my trouble I will call upon you, for you will answer me.
-- Psalm 86:6, 7

I cried to God with my voice, even to God with my voice, and he gave ear to me.
-- Psalm 77:1

I love the LORD, because he has heard my voice and my supplications. Because he has inclined his ear to me, therefore will I call upon him as long as I live.
-- Psalm 116:1, 2

And it shall come to pass that before they call, I will answer. And while they are yet speaking, I will hear.
-- Isaiah 65:24

The sacrifice of the wicked is an abomination to the LORD, but the prayer of the upright is his delight.
-- Proverbs 15:8

The LORD is far from the wicked, but he hears the prayer of the righteous.
-- Proverbs 15:29

I sought the LORD, and he heard me and delivered me from all my fears.

This poor man cried, and the LORD heard him and saved him out of all his troubles.

The eyes of the LORD are upon the righteous, and his ears are open unto their cry.

The righteous cry, and the LORD hears and delivers them out of all their troubles.

-- Psalm 34:4, 6, 15, 17

And this is the confidence that we have in him, that, if we ask anything according to his will, he hears us: and if we know that he hears us, whatever we ask, we know that we have the petitions that we desired of him.

-- I John 5:14, 15

I have called upon you, for you will hear me, O God. Incline your ear to me, and hear my speech.

-- Psalm 17:6

For I said in my haste, "I am cut off from before your eyes!" Nevertheless, you heard the voice of my supplications when I cried to you.

-- Psalm 31:22

In my distress I called upon the LORD and cried to my God, and he heard my voice from his temple, and my cry entered into his ears.

-- 2 Samuel 22:7

Blessed be the LORD, because he has heard the voice of my supplications.

-- Psalm 28:6

I cried to the LORD with my voice, and he heard me from his holy hill.
    -- Psalm 3:4

LORD, you have heard the desire of the humble. You will prepare their heart; you will cause your ear to hear.
    -- Psalm 10:17

But know that the LORD has set apart him who is godly for himself. The LORD will hear when I call to him.
    -- Psalm 4:3

The LORD has heard my supplication; the LORD will receive my prayer.
    -- Psalm 6:9

… He does not forget the cry of the humble.
    -- Psalm 9:12

He will regard the prayer of the destitute and not despise their prayer.
    -- Psalm 102:17

Then shall you call upon me, and you shall go and pray to me, and I will hearken to you.
    -- Jeremiah 29:12

For he has not despised nor abhorred the affliction of the afflicted; neither has he hid his face from him; but when he cried to him, he heard.
    -- Psalm 22:24

… I cried because of my affliction to the LORD, and he heard me; from out of the belly of hell I cried, and you heard my voice.

When my soul fainted within me, I remembered the LORD: and my prayer came in to you, into your holy temple.
-- Jonah 2:2, 7

In my distress I called upon the LORD and cried to my God. He heard my voice from his temple, and my cry came before him, even into his ears.
-- Psalm 18:6

For in you, O LORD, do I hope: you will hear, O Lord my God.
-- Psalm 38:15

You shall make your prayer unto him, and he shall hear you
….
-- Job 22:27

I will praise you, for you have heard me and have become my salvation.
-- Psalm 118:21

… For I have mercy upon them, and they shall be as though I had not cast them off: for I am the LORD their God and will hear them.
-- Zechariah 10:6

The Lord Answers Your Prayers

We have been establishing that God is in the business of answering our prayers. The following verses are even more clear on this truth than the ones in the previous chapter. Meditate on them, and as you do, you will transfer their reality from the written page to the pages of your heart. Once you know in your heart that God desires to answer you, there is no stopping what He can use you to accomplish for His Kingdom through your intercessions.

I called upon the LORD in distress: the LORD answered me, and set me in a large place.
-- Psalm 118:5

And it shall come to pass that before they call, I will answer. And while they are yet speaking, I will hear.
-- Isaiah 65:24

In the day of my trouble I will call upon you, for you will answer me.
-- Psalm 86:7

Moses and Aaron among his priests, and Samuel among those who call upon his name; they called upon the LORD, and he answered them.
-- Psalm 99:6

You called in trouble, and I delivered you; I answered you in the secret place of thunder....
-- Psalm 81:7

In the day when I cried, you answered me and strengthened me with strength in my soul.
  -- Psalm 138:3

Call to me, and I will answer you, and I will show you great and mighty things, which you do not yet know.
  -- Jeremiah 33:3

Because he has set his love upon me, therefore I will deliver him. I will set him on high, because he has known my name. *He shall call upon me, and I will answer him.* I will be with him in trouble; I will deliver him and honor him.
  -- Psalm 91:14, 15 (Italics mine)

And this is the confidence that we have in him, that, if we ask anything according to his will, he hears us. And if we know that he hears us, whatever we ask, we know that we have the petitions that we desired of him.
  -- I John 5:14, 15

And so, after he [Abraham] had patiently endured, he obtained the promise.
  -- Hebrews 6:15

And whatever we ask we receive of him, because we keep his commandments and do those things which are pleasing in his sight.
  -- I John 3:21

And all things whatever you shall ask in prayer, believing, you shall receive.
  -- Matthew 21:22

Therefore I say to you, whatever things you desire, when you pray, believe that you receive them, and you shall have them.
   -- Mark 11:24

The LORD is near to all of them who call upon him, to all who call upon him in truth. He will fulfill the desire of those who fear him; he will also hear their cry and will save them.
   -- Psalm 145:18, 19

You have given him his heart's desire and have not withheld the request of his lips.
   -- Psalm 21:2

... He will be very gracious to you at the voice of your cry; when he shall hear it, he will answer you.
   -- Isaiah 30:19

Then shall you call, and the LORD shall answer; you shall cry, and he shall say, "Here I am."
   -- Isaiah 58:9

And whatever you shall ask in my name, that I will do, that the Father may be glorified in the Son. If you shall ask anything in my name, I will do it.
   -- John 14:13, 14

Ask, and it shall be given to you; seek, and you shall find; knock, and it shall be opened to you: for everyone who asks receives; and he who seeks finds; and to him who knocks it shall be opened.
   -- Matthew 7:7, 8

Praying for Specific Needs

Health and Healing

Many wrong teachings about health and sickness have developed through the centuries within the Church to accommodate our unbelief. The truth is, health and healing are our inheritance under both the Old and New Covenants. Jesus paid a terrible price not only for our salvation from sin, but also for our healing and deliverance, and He wants us to have what He paid for. The Bible is very clear on God's desire to heal. God does not have favorites that He is willing to heal, and those not so favored whom He will not.

Like many other blessings that He promises in His Word, healing does not always manifest instantaneously. It can, but when it does not, we tend to think that nothing happened when we prayed. The key is to continue to press the issue in prayer, believing that the healing we are praying for is already ours positionally in heaven. We must insist on it until the answer manifests for all to see.

These verses will help you to win the healing battles that you face:

Hope in God: for I shall yet praise him, who is the health of my countenance and my God.
-- Psalm 42:11 and Psalm 43:5

Who forgives all your iniquities; who heals all your diseases.
-- Psalm 103:3

O LORD my God, I cried unto you, and you have healed me.
-- Psalm 30:2

Beloved, I wish above all things that you may prosper and be in health, even as your soul prospers.
-- 3 John 2

Surely he shall deliver you from the snare of the fowler and from the loathsome pestilence.
-- Psalm 91:3

He will keep you safe from all hidden dangers and from all deadly diseases.
-- Psalm 91:3 (Good News for Modern Man)

Because you have made the LORD, who is my refuge, even the Most High, your habitation, there shall no evil befall you, neither shall any plague come near your dwelling.
-- Psalm 91:9, 10

Uphold me according to your word, that I may live: and let me not be ashamed of my hope.
-- Psalm 119:116

And these signs shall follow them who believe: in my name they shall cast out devils; they shall speak with new tongues; they shall take up serpents; and if they drink any deadly thing, it shall not hurt them; they shall lay hands on the sick, and they shall recover.
-- Mark 16:17, 18

But he was wounded for our transgressions; he was bruised for our iniquities. The chastisement of our peace was upon him, and with his stripes we are healed.
-- Isaiah 53:5

… By whose stripes you were healed.
-- I Peter 2:24

… [Jesus] healed all who were sick, that it might be fulfilled which was spoken by Isaiah the prophet, "He himself took our infirmities and bore our sicknesses."
-- Matthew 8:16, 17

Is anyone sick among you? Let him call for the elders of the church, and let them pray over him, anointing him with oil in the name of the Lord. And the prayer of faith shall save the sick, and the Lord shall raise him up. And if he has committed sins, they shall be forgiven him. Confess your faults to each other and pray for each other, so that you may be healed. The effective, fervent prayer of a righteous man avails much.
-- James 5:14-16

If you will diligently hearken to the voice of the LORD your God, and will do what is right in his sight, and will give ear to his commandments, and keep all his statutes, I will not put any of these diseases upon you which I have brought upon the Egyptians: for I am the LORD who heals you.
-- Exodus 15:26

Many are the afflictions of the righteous, but the LORD delivers him out of them all.
-- Psalm 34:19

Because he has set his love upon me, therefore I will deliver him. … With long life I will satisfy him and show him my salvation.
-- Psalm 91:14-16

Blessed is he who considers the poor: the LORD will deliver him in time of trouble. The LORD will preserve him, and keep him alive, and he shall be blessed upon the earth. And you will not deliver him to the will of his enemies. *The LORD will strengthen him upon the bed of languishing; you will make his bed in his sickness.*
     -- Psalm 41:1-3 (Italics mine)

The LORD will sustain him on his sickbed and restore him from his bed of illness.
     -- Psalm 41:3 (NIV)

He sent his word, and healed them, and delivered them from their destructions.
     -- Psalm 107:20

Heal me, O LORD, and I shall be healed; save me, and I shall be saved: for you are my praise.
     -- Jeremiah 17:14

But to you who fear my name the Sun of righteousness shall arise with healing in his wings: and you shall go forth and grow up as calves of the stall.
     -- Malachi 4:2

You shall not bow down to their gods, nor serve them, nor do according to their works. … And you shall serve the LORD your God, and he shall bless your bread and your water, and I will take sickness away from the midst of you. Nothing shall cast its young, nor be barren, in your land. The number of your days I will fulfill.
     -- Exodus 23:24-26

... And as many as touched him [Jesus] were made whole.
-- Mark 6:56

... And great multitudes followed him [Jesus], and he healed them all.
-- Matthew 12:15

And the LORD will take away from you all sickness and will not put any of the evil diseases of Egypt, which you know, upon you, but will lay them upon all those who hate you.
-- Deuteronomy 7:15

Then shall your light break forth as the morning, and your health shall spring forth speedily. And your righteousness shall go before you; the glory of the Lord shall be your rearward.
-- Isaiah 58:8 (To understand properly, start reading at verse 6.)

The LORD is your keeper; the LORD is your shade upon your right hand. *The sun shall not smite you by day*, nor the moon by night.
-- Psalm 121:5,6 (Use to declare protection from skin cancer. Italics mine.)

The following Scripture verses do not directly speak of healing, but can be used with confidence in relation to your need for healing:

... For your heavenly Father knows that you have need of all these things. But seek first the kingdom of God and his righteousness, and all these things shall be added to you.
-- Matthew 6:32, 33

... Is my hand shortened at all that it cannot redeem? Or have I no power to deliver? Behold, at my rebuke I dry up the sea ....
     -- Isaiah 50:2

Ask, and it shall be given to you; seek, and you shall find; knock, and it shall be opened to you: for everyone who asks receives; and he who seeks finds; and to him who knocks it shall be opened. For what man is there among you, whom, if his son asks bread, he will give him a stone? Or if he asks a fish, will he give him a serpent? If you then, being evil, know how to give good gifts to your children, how much more shall your Father who is in heaven give good things to those who ask him?
     -- Matthew 7:7-11

Therefore I say to you, whatever things you desire, when you pray, believe that you receive them, and you shall have them.
     -- Mark 11:24

But my God shall supply all your need according to his riches in glory by Christ Jesus.
     -- Philippians 4:19

Jesus Christ the same yesterday, and today, and forever.
     -- Hebrews 13:8

But you, beloved, building up yourselves on your most holy faith, praying in the Holy Spirit.
     -- Jude 20 (Pray in tongues to build your faith and health. See *The Power of Your Prayer Language* in my book, *The Intercessor Manual*.)

He who spared not his own Son, but delivered him up for us all, how shall he not with him also freely give us all things?
   -- Romans 8:32

Prosperity

A good father desires for his children to have their needs met -- and not just at a notch above starvation. He wants his children to not only have the bare minimum, but he goes beyond that to give them many gifts -- just because he loves to delight them.

Our heavenly Father is not stingy with us, either. What any good earthly dad would do for his children, God the Father will do to a higher degree. Jesus said, "*If you then, being evil, know how to give good gifts to your children, how much more shall your Father who is in heaven give good things to those who ask him?*" (Matthew 7:11).

Our part is to understand that prosperity is God's plan for us and to therefore appropriate it into our lives. It does not glorify God to have His beloved children unable to pay their bills or to be living in a bankrupt condition!

Perhaps you or someone you love is having financial difficulties. It may be because of poor stewardship in the past -- or it may be through no fault of your own at all. When we do what we can to use what He has given us responsibly from this point on, and when we put His Kingdom before our own desires, we can be assured that He will take care of us and that He will restore our finances to what they should be.

Here are some verses to help you pray through to financial victory:

Beloved, I wish above all things that you may prosper and be in health, even as your soul prospers.
   -- 3 John 2

... Blessed is the man who fears the LORD, who greatly delights in his commandments. His seed [descendants] shall be mighty upon earth; the generation of the upright shall be blessed. Wealth and riches shall be in his house, and his righteousness shall endure forever.
-- Psalm 112:1-3

But you shall remember the LORD your God, for it is he who gives you power to get wealth, so that he may establish his covenant which he swore to your fathers, as it is this day.
-- Deuteronomy 8:18

... No good thing will he withhold from those who walk uprightly.
-- Psalm 84:11

He who did not spare his own Son, but delivered him up for us all, shall he not with him also freely give us all things?
-- Romans 8:32

O fear the LORD, you who are his saints, for there is no want to them who fear him. The young lions lack and suffer hunger, but they who seek the LORD shall not want any good thing.
-- Psalm 34:9, 10

... The upright shall have good things in possession.
-- Proverbs 28:10

The LORD, your Redeemer, the Holy One of Israel, says this: "I am the LORD your God who teaches you to profit, who leads you by the way that you should go."
-- Isaiah 48:17

For the needy shall not always be forgotten; the expectation of the poor shall not perish forever.
-- Psalm 9:18

I have been young and now am old, yet I have not seen the righteous forsaken, nor his seed begging for bread.
-- Psalm 37:25

For every beast of the forest is mine and the cattle upon a thousand hills.
-- Psalm 50:10

But seek first the kingdom of God and his righteousness, and all these things shall be added to you.
-- Matthew 6:33 (See Matthew 6:25-34.)

He who has a bountiful [generous] eye shall be blessed, for he gives of his bread to the poor.
-- Proverbs 22:9

If then God so clothes the grass, which is today in the field and tomorrow is cast into the oven, how much more will he clothe you, O you of little faith? And do not seek what you shall eat, or what you shall drink, neither be of doubtful mind. For all these things do the nations of the world seek after -- and your Father knows that you have need of these things. But rather, seek the kingdom of God, and all these things shall be added to you.
-- Luke 12:28-31 (See Luke 12:22-31.)

By humility and the fear of the LORD are riches, and honor, and life.
-- Proverbs 22:4

The LORD is my shepherd: I shall not want.

He makes me lie down in green pastures; he leads me beside the still waters.

You prepare a table before me in the presence of my enemies. You anoint my head with oil; my cup runs over.

Surely goodness and mercy shall follow me all the days of my life, and I will dwell in the house of the LORD forever.
    -- Psalm 23:1, 2, 5, 6

Your kingdom come. Your will be done in earth as it is in heaven. Give us this day our daily bread.
    -- Matthew 6:10, 11

Give us day by day our daily bread.
    -- Luke 11:3

Behold, the eye of the LORD is upon them who fear him, upon them who hope in his mercy, to deliver their souls from death and to keep them alive in famine.
    -- Psalm 33:18, 19

The LORD knows the days of the upright, and their inheritance shall be forever. They shall not be ashamed in the evil time, and in the days of famine they shall be satisfied.
    -- Psalm 37:18, 19

And the [threshing] floors shall be full of wheat, and the vats shall overflow with wine and oil. And I will restore to you the years that the locust has eaten. ... And you shall eat in plenty, and be satisfied, and praise the name of the LORD your God, who has dealt wondrously with you: and my people shall never be ashamed.
    -- Joel 2:24-26 (Read Joel 2:21-27 for the full picture.)

Trust in the LORD and do good; so shall you dwell in the land, and most certainly you shall be fed.
-- Psalm 37:3

And the LORD turned the captivity of Job when he prayed for his friends. Also, the LORD gave Job twice as much as he had before. Then there came to him all his brethren, and all his sisters, and all who had been in his acquaintance before, and … every man also gave him a piece of money, and every one an earring of gold. So the LORD blessed the latter end of Job more than his beginning ….
-- Job 42:10-12

Save now, I beseech you, O LORD: O LORD, I beseech you, send prosperity now.
-- Psalm 118.25

The eyes of all wait upon you, and you give them their food in due season. You open your hand and satisfy the desire of every living thing.
-- Psalm 145:15, 16

He who tills his land shall have plenty of bread, but he who follows after vain persons shall have poverty enough.

A faithful man shall abound with blessings, but he who makes haste to be rich shall not be innocent.

He who hastes to be rich has an evil eye and does not consider that poverty shall come upon him.

He who gives to the poor shall not lack, but he who hides his eyes shall have many a curse.
-- Proverbs 28:19, 20, 22, 27

The LORD will not suffer the soul of the righteous to famish, but he casts away the substance of the wicked.
-- Proverbs 10:3

The thief comes only to steal, and to kill, and to destroy: I am come that they might have life and that they might have it more abundantly.
-- John 10:10

The sowing and reaping principle:

... He who sows sparingly shall also reap sparingly, and he who sows bountifully shall also reap bountifully.

And God is able to make all grace abound toward you, so that you, always having all sufficiency in all things, may abound to every good work.

Now may he who ministers seed to the sower both minister bread for your food and multiply your seed sown, and increase the fruits of your righteousness, being enriched in everything to all bountifulness, which causes through us thanksgiving to God.
-- 2 Corinthians 9:6, 8, 10-11

Give, and it shall be given to you: good measure, pressed down, and shaken together, and running over, shall men give into your bosom. For with the same measure with which you mete [give out] it shall be measured to you again.
-- Luke 6:38

Cast your bread upon the waters, for you shall find it after many days.
-- Ecclesiastes 11:1

There is one who scatters [his wealth] and yet increases, and there is one who withholds more than is right, but it tends toward poverty. The generous soul shall be made fat [filled with abundance], and he who waters shall also be watered himself. He who withholds corn shall the people curse, but blessing shall be upon the head of him who sells it.

    -- Proverbs 11:24-26

But my God shall supply all your need according to his riches in glory by Christ Jesus.

    -- Philippians 4:19 (To be correctly understood, read in context, starting with v. 15.)

Bring all the tithes into the storehouse, that there may be food in my house, and prove me now with this, says the LORD of hosts, if I will not open for you the windows of heaven, and pour out upon you a blessing, that there shall not be room enough to receive it. And I will rebuke the devourer for your sakes, and he shall not destroy the fruits of your ground; neither shall your vine cast her fruit before the time in the field, says the LORD of hosts. And all nations shall call you blessed: for you shall be a delightsome land, says the LORD of hosts.

    -- Malachi 3:10-12

Salvation for Loved Ones

It is God's will for all people to know Him. Will everyone come to that knowledge and embrace Jesus as their Savior? No, although it would be to God's delight if they did. There is a seeming conflict between the "whosoever will" truth and the equal truth of being foreordained and "elect." Both doctrines are part of the whole picture of God's plan for mankind, a mystery beyond our limited understanding.

What we can be sure of, is that if we pray for someone's salvation, we are praying according to God's perfect will for that person's life, and, 1 John 5:14, 15 tells us, *"And this is the confidence that we have in him, that, if we ask anything according to his will, he hears us. And if we know that he hears us, whatever we ask, we know that we have the petitions that we desired of him."* In praying for people's salvations, we are partnering with the Lord to bring them into their place among the children of God. We do not have to doubt; we can rest assured that as we persevere, God will surely turn their hearts to Him.

The hardest heart cannot withstand the prayers of an earnest intercessor. Persist, and you will see that heart changed by the Holy Spirit's miraculous activity upon it. What a privilege we have in praying lost souls into the Kingdom!

I have listed the following verses to build your understanding that God truly does provide for every person's salvation. You will also find a few verses that will help you strategically pray for and decree those salvations into existence. Use the verses in some of the other chapters of this guide as well, to assert your claims on heaven and to see God's promises of salvation fulfilled.

The Lord is not slack concerning his promise, as some men count slackness; but is longsuffering toward us, not willing that any should perish, but that all should come to repentance.
-- 2 Peter 3:9

For God so loved the world, that he gave his only begotten Son, that whoever believes in him should not perish, but have everlasting life. For God did not send his Son into the world to condemn the world, but that the world through him might be saved.
-- John 3:16, 17

I exhort therefore, that, first of all, supplications, prayers, intercessions, and giving of thanks be made for all men.
For this is good and acceptable in the sight of God our Savior, who wills for all men to be saved and to come to the knowledge of the truth.
-- 1 Timothy 2:1, 3, 4

… The man Christ Jesus, who gave himself a ransom for *all*, to be testified in due time.
-- 1 Timothy 2:5, 6 (Italics mine)

For the grace of God that brings salvation has appeared to all men.
-- Titus 2:11

For whoever shall call upon the name of the Lord shall be saved.
-- Romans 10:13

And it shall come to pass, that whoever shall call on the name of the LORD shall be delivered ….
-- Joel 2:32

For the Son of man is come to seek and to save that which was lost.
    -- Luke 19:10

I say to you, that likewise joy shall be in heaven over one sinner who repents, more than over ninety-nine just persons who need no repentance.
Likewise, I say to you that there is joy in the presence of the angels of God over one sinner who repents.
    -- Luke 15:7, 10

I am sought by them that did not ask for me; I am found by those who did not seek me .... I have spread out my hands all day long to a rebellious people, who walk in a way which is not good, after their own thoughts.
    -- Isaiah 65:1, 2 (They will begin to seek Jesus as we pray for them.)

... I was found by those who did not seek me; I was made manifest [revealed] to those who did not ask about me.
    -- Romans 10:20

Who has delivered us from the power of darkness, and has translated us into the kingdom of his dear Son. In whom we have redemption through his blood, even the forgiveness of sins.
    -- Colossians 1:13, 14

A new heart also will I give you, and a new spirit will I put within you. And I will take away the stony heart out of your flesh, and I will give you a heart of flesh [a softened heart].
    -- Ezekiel 36:26

Not by works of righteousness which we have done, but according to his mercy he saved us, by the washing of regeneration [rebirth; restoration], and renewing of the Holy Spirit, which he shed on us abundantly through Jesus Christ our Savior, so that being justified by his grace, we should be made heirs according to the hope of eternal life.
    -- Titus 3:5-7

... And the Lord added to the church daily such as should be saved.
    -- Acts 2:47

But this shall be the covenant that I will make with the house of Israel. After those days, says the LORD, I will put my law in their inner parts, and write it in their hearts, and will be their God, and they shall be my people. And they shall teach no more every man his neighbor and every man his brother, saying, "Know the LORD." For they shall all know me, from the least of them to the greatest of them, says the LORD, for I will forgive their iniquity, and I will remember their sin no more.
    -- Jeremiah 31:33, 34 (Use to pray for a Great Awakening.)

For Family:

... But as for me and my house, we will serve the LORD.
    -- Joshua 24:15

Train up a child in the way he should go: and when he is old, he will not depart from it.
    -- Proverbs 22:6

... Believe on the Lord Jesus Christ, and you shall be saved, *and your house.*
    -- Acts 16:31 (Italics mine)

Fear not, for I am with you. I will bring your seed from the east, and gather you from the west. I will say to the north, "Give up!" and to the south, "Do not keep back!" Bring my sons from afar, and my daughters from the ends of the earth -- even every one that is called by my name. For I have created him for my glory; I have formed him; yes, I have made him.
    -- Isaiah 43:5-7 (Call the prodigals home, and declare God's purposes over them.)

For this son of mine was dead and is alive again; he was lost and is found ....
    -- Luke 15:24 (Use as a decree, to call in the prodigal.)

Israel

Israel: God's beloved people. Deuteronomy 32:10 and Zechariah 2:8 refer to them as the apple of God's eye. God promised Abraham, "*I will bless those who bless you, and curse him who curses you*" (Genesis 12:3). This promise was extended down through Abraham's family line through Isaac and Jacob (Israel), to whom God promised, "*In you and in your seed shall all the families of the earth be blessed*" (Genesis 28:14).

It is a very wise thing to get on God's bandwagon and bless those whom He blesses! The following Scriptures will help you partner in prayer with the Father's heart for His people Israel:

For Salvation:

But this shall be the covenant that I will make with the house of Israel. After those days, says the LORD, I will put my law in their inner parts, and write it in their hearts, and will be their God, and they shall be my people. And they shall teach no more every man his neighbor and every man his brother, saying, "Know the LORD." For they shall all know me, from the least of them to the greatest of them, says the LORD, for I will forgive their iniquity, and I will remember their sin no more.
    -- Jeremiah 31:33, 34

Isaiah also cries concerning Israel, "Though the number of the children of Israel is as the sand of the sea, *a remnant shall be saved.*"
    -- Romans 9:27 (Italics mine)

Brethren, my heart's desire and prayer to God for Israel is that they might be saved.
  -- Romans 10:1

And they also, if they do not still abide in unbelief, shall be grafted in: for God is able to graft them in again.
  -- Romans 11:23

And so all Israel shall be saved, as it is written, "There shall come out of Zion the Deliverer and shall turn away ungodliness from Jacob, for this is my covenant to them, when I shall take away their sins."
  -- Romans 11:26, 27 (Read Romans 9-11 for understanding of God's plan for Israel's salvation.)

But their [Israel's] minds were blinded: for until this day the same veil remains untaken away in the reading of the Old Testament, which veil is done away in Christ. But even to this day, when Moses is read, the veil is upon their hearts. Nevertheless, when their hearts shall turn to the Lord, the veil shall be taken away.
  -- 2 Corinthians 3:14-16 (For best understanding, begin reading at 2 Corinthians 3:7.)

For he is our peace, who has made both [Gentile and Jew] one, and has broken down the middle wall of partition between us ... to make in himself of the two one new man, so making peace, and that he might reconcile both [Gentile and Jew] to God in one body by the cross ....
  -- Ephesians 2:14-16

And they shall call them "the holy people, the redeemed of the LORD" ....
  -- Isaiah 62:12

And I will pour upon the house of David, and upon the inhabitants of Jerusalem, the spirit of grace and of supplications. And they shall look upon him whom they have pierced, and they shall mourn for him, as one mourns for his only son, and shall be in bitterness for him, as one that is in bitterness for his firstborn.

In that day there shall be a fountain opened to the house of David and to the inhabitants of Jerusalem for sin and for uncleanness.

  -- Zechariah 12:10 and 13:1

For Zion's sake I will not hold my peace, and for Jerusalem's sake I will not rest, until the righteousness thereof goes forth as brightness, and the salvation thereof as a lamp that burns.

  -- Isaiah 62:1

For Protection:

Pray for the peace of Jerusalem; they shall prosper that love you. Peace be within your walls, and prosperity within your palaces. For my brethren and companions' sakes, I will now say, "Peace be within you."

  -- Psalm 122:6-8

They who trust in the LORD shall be as mount Zion, which cannot be removed, but abides forever.

As the mountains are round about Jerusalem, so the LORD is round about his people from henceforth, even forever.

As for such as turn aside to their crooked ways, the LORD shall lead them forth with the workers of iniquity: but peace shall be upon Israel.

  -- Psalm 125:1, 2, 5

I have set watchmen upon your walls, O Jerusalem, which shall never hold their peace, day or night. You who make mention of the LORD, do not keep silence.
-- Isaiah 62:6

O Israel, trust in the LORD. He is their help and their shield.
-- Psalm 115:9

... Jerusalem shall be inhabited as towns without walls for the multitude of men and cattle therein. "For I," says the LORD, "will be to her a wall of fire round about, and will be the glory in the midst of her."
-- Zechariah 2:4, 5

For Her Glorious Establishment:

Now, if the fall of them causes the riches of the world, and the diminishing of them the riches of the Gentiles, how much more their fullness?

For if the casting away of them causes the reconciling of the world, what shall the receiving of them be, but life from the dead?
-- Romans 11:12, 15

For Zion's sake I will not hold my peace, and for Jerusalem's sake I will not rest, until the righteousness thereof goes forth as brightness, and the salvation thereof as a lamp that burns. And the Gentiles shall see your righteousness, and all kings your glory. And you shall be called by a new name, which the mouth of the LORD shall name. You shall also be a crown of glory in the hand of the LORD and a royal diadem in the hand of your God.
-- Isaiah 62:1-3

And give him no rest, until he establishes and until he makes Jerusalem a praise in the earth.

   -- Isaiah 62:7 (See all of Isaiah 62 for a fuller picture.)

Praise the LORD, O Jerusalem; praise your God, O Zion. For he has strengthened the bars of your gates; he has blessed your children within you. He makes peace in your borders and fills you with the finest of the wheat.

   -- Psalm 147:12-14

Sing and rejoice, O daughter of Zion, for look, I come, and I will dwell in the midst of you, says the LORD. And many nations shall be joined to the LORD in that day and shall be my people. And I will dwell in the midst of you, and you shall know that the LORD of hosts has sent me to you. And the LORD shall inherit Judah, his portion, in the holy land and shall choose Jerusalem again.

   -- Zechariah 2:10-12

Our Nation

We look for a Great Awakening which will span the globe -- a final harvest that will precede end-time events and the return of Jesus. Some nations, especially in the third world, are already experiencing it, but many nations are not -- yet.

It is our responsibility as intercessors to pick up our mantle to pray it in. Awakening of the magnitude we look for is a sovereign move of God. But "sovereign" moves are nearly always brought about by prayer -- prayer that has been implanted by the Holy Spirit into the hearts of faithful intercessors, who hear the heartbeat of God and respond. Our participation, our partnering with Him, will bring the plans of God into reality in the earth, and particularly, into the nation in which we live.

The following verses will aid you in praying for our nation's leaders, for mercy, for a return of righteousness, and for awakening:

For Leaders:

I exhort therefore that, first of all, supplications, prayers, intercessions, and giving of thanks be made for all men -- for kings, and for all that are in authority, so that we may lead a quiet and peaceable life in all godliness and honesty. For this is good and acceptable in the sight of God our Savior, who will have all men to be saved and to come to the knowledge of the truth.
-- 1 Timothy 2:1-4

The king's heart is in the hand of the LORD, as the rivers of water; he turns it wherever he wills.
-- Proverbs 21:1

Take away the wicked from before the king, and his throne shall be established in righteousness.
-- Proverbs 25:5

It is an abomination to kings to commit wickedness, for the throne is established by righteousness.
-- Proverbs 16:12

By judgment the king establishes the land, but he who receives gifts overthrows it.
-- Proverbs 29:4

Mercy and truth preserve the king, and his throne is upheld by mercy.
-- Proverbs 20:28

Repentance and Beseeching for Mercy:

Righteousness exalts a nation, but sin is a reproach to any people.
-- Proverbs 14:34

If my people, who are called by my name, will humble themselves, and pray, and seek my face, and turn from their wicked ways, then I will hear from heaven, and will forgive their sin, and will heal their land.
-- 2 Chronicles 7:14

And I set my face to the Lord God, to seek by prayer and supplications, with fasting, and sackcloth, and ashes. And I prayed to the LORD my God, and made my confession, and said, "O Lord, the great and dreadful God, keeping the covenant and mercy to those who love him, and to those who keep his commandments:

"We have sinned, and have committed iniquity, and have done wickedly, and have rebelled, even by departing from your precepts and from your judgments. Neither have we heeded your servants the prophets, who spoke in your name to our kings, our princes, and our fathers, and to all the people of the land.

"O Lord, confusion of face belongs to us: to our kings, to our princes, and to our fathers, because we have sinned against you. To the Lord our God belong mercies and forgiveness, though we have rebelled against him. Neither have we obeyed the voice of the LORD our God to walk in his laws, which he set before us by his servants the prophets.

"All this evil has come upon us: yet we did not pray to the LORD our God, that we might turn from our iniquities, and understand your truth. And now, O Lord our God ... we have sinned, we have done wickedly.

"O Lord, according to all your righteousness I beseech you: let your anger and your fury be turned away ... because for our sins, and for the iniquities of our fathers, ... your people have become a reproach to all who are about us.

"Now therefore, O our God, hear the prayer of your servant and his supplications, and cause your face to shine upon your sanctuary that is desolate, for the Lord's sake. O my God, incline your ear and hear; open your eyes and behold our desolations, ... for we do not present our supplications before you for our righteousness, but because of your great

mercies. O Lord, hear; O Lord, forgive; O Lord, hearken and do; do not defer, for your own sake, O my God ...."
-- Daniel 9:3-6, 8-10, 13, 15-19

And I sought for a man among them, that would make up the hedge and stand in the gap before me for the land, that I would not destroy it: but I found none.
-- Ezekiel 22:30

And Judah gathered themselves together to ask for help from the LORD; even out of all the cities of Judah they came to seek the LORD.
-- 2 Chronicles 20:4 (illustrates the importance of coming together in corporate prayer)

For Righteous Submission to the Lord Jesus:

All nations whom you have made shall come and worship before you, O Lord, and shall glorify your name.
-- Psalm 86:9

... The kingdoms of this world have now become the kingdoms of our Lord and of his Christ, and he shall reign forever and ever.
-- Revelation 11:15

Wherefore God also has highly exalted him, and given him a name which is above every name, that at the name of Jesus every knee should bow, of things in heaven, and things in earth, and things under the earth, and that every tongue should confess that Jesus Christ is Lord, to the glory of God the Father.
-- Philippians 2:9-11 (Decree that our nation shall bow the knee to Jesus and honor Him.)

Yes, all kings shall fall down before him; all nations shall serve him.
-- Psalm 72:11

For a Great Awakening:

... Awake you who sleep, and arise from the dead, and Christ shall give you light.
-- Ephesians 5:14

Arise, shine: for your light has come, and the glory of the LORD is risen upon you. For, behold, the darkness shall cover the earth, and gross darkness the people, but the LORD shall arise upon you, and his glory shall be seen upon you. And the Gentiles shall come to your light, and kings to the brightness of your rising.
-- Isaiah 60:1-3

A new heart also will I give you, and a new spirit will I put within you. And I will take away the stony heart out of your flesh, and I will give you a heart of flesh [softened heart].
-- Ezekiel 36:26

... And the Lord added to the church daily such as should be saved.
-- Acts 2:47

... The harvest truly is great, but the laborers are few: pray, therefore, to the Lord of the harvest, that he would send forth laborers into his harvest.
-- Luke 10:2

That all the people of the earth may know that the LORD is God and that there is no other.
    -- 1 Kings 8:60

For the earth shall be filled with the knowledge of the glory of the LORD, as the waters cover the sea.
    -- Habakkuk 2:14

Your Pastor (Ministry Leaders, Missionaries)

This chapter is intensely dear to my heart, for my primary function as an intercessor is to uphold my pastor, who is also an apostle, in prayer. Many of you have a similar longing or calling.

Christian ministry leaders have a target on their backs, so to speak. They need our continual prayer covering to keep them from spiritual attack. They also need our intercession to prepare the way in the heavenlies so that they can receive God's strategies for their church flocks or other ministries they lead. For greater understanding of this vital prayer ministry toward pastors, please see my book, *The Intercessor Manual*, which can be purchased from Full Gospel Family Publications.

Here are some verses to help you pray effectively for your pastor or ministry leader. They also apply well to missionaries:

Open Doors to Proclaim the Gospel:

... Pray also for us, that God would open to us a door of utterance to speak the mystery of Christ, ... that I may make it manifest, as I ought to speak.
    -- Colossians 4:3, 4

Finally, brethren, pray for us, that the word of the Lord may have free course and be glorified, even as it is with you.
    -- 2 Thessalonians 3:1

For a great and effectual door is opened to me, and there are many adversaries.
    -- 1 Corinthians 16:9

... These things says he who is holy, he who is true, he who has the key of David, he who opens and no man shuts; and shuts and no man opens: "I know your works. Behold, I have set before you an open door, and no man can shut it: for you have a little strength, and have kept my word, and have not denied my name."
-- Revelation 3:7, 8

[Pray] for me, that utterance may be given to me, that I may open my mouth boldly, to make known the mystery of the gospel, ... that therein I may speak boldly, as I ought to speak.
-- Ephesians 6:19, 20

For Financial Provision (see also the *Prosperity* chapter):

Even so has the Lord ordained that they who preach the gospel should live of the gospel.
-- 1 Corinthians 9:14

Let the elders that rule well be counted worthy of double honor [compensation], especially they who labor in the word and doctrine. For the Scripture says, "You shall not muzzle the ox that treads out the corn," and, "The laborer is worthy of his reward."
-- 1 Timothy 5:17, 18

Let him who is taught in the word communicate [give] to him who teaches in all good things.
-- Galatians 6:6

The husbandman [farmer] who labors must be first partaker of the fruits.
-- 2 Timothy 2:6

That They Would Be Respected:

And we beseech you, brethren, to know those who labor among you, and are over you in the Lord, and admonish you, and to esteem them very highly in love for their work's sake ....
> -- 1 Thessalonians 5:12, 13

Obey those who have the rule over you, and submit yourselves. For they watch for your souls, as they who must give account, that they may do it with joy, and not with grief, for that is unprofitable for you.
> -- Hebrews 13:17

Render therefore to all their dues: tribute to whom tribute is due; custom to whom custom; fear to whom fear; *honor to whom honor.*
> -- Romans 13:7 (Italics mine)

That They Would Be Effective Ministers:

But speak the things which are becoming to sound doctrine.
> -- Titus 2:1

Study [be diligent] to show yourself approved to God, a workman that does not need to be ashamed, rightly dividing the word of truth.
> -- 2 Timothy 2:15

Not that we are sufficient of ourselves to think anything as of ourselves; but our sufficiency is of God, who also has made us able ministers of the new testament....
> -- 2 Corinthians 3:5, 6

And the servant of the Lord must not strive, but be gentle to all men, apt to teach, patient, in meekness instructing those who oppose themselves ....

   -- 2 Timothy 2:24, 25

And my speech and my preaching was not with enticing words of man's wisdom, but in demonstration of the Spirit and of power, that your faith would not stand in the wisdom of men, but in the power of God.

   -- 1 Corinthians 2:4, 5

Preach the word; be instant in season, out of season; reprove, rebuke, exhort with all long-suffering and doctrine.

But watch in all things, endure afflictions, do the work of an evangelist, make full proof of your ministry.

   -- 2 Timothy 4:3, 5

Let your speech be always with grace, seasoned with salt, that you may know how you ought to answer every man.

   -- Colossians 4:6

But we will give ourselves to prayer, and to the ministry of the word.

   -- Acts 6:4

Feed the flock of God which is among you, taking the oversight thereof -- not by constraint, but willingly; not for filthy lucre [profit], but having a ready mind, neither as being lords over God's heritage, but being examples to the flock.

   -- 1 Peter 5:2, 3

For Spiritual Protection (see also Chapter 12, *Our God Is Our Safety*):

... But he who is begotten of God keeps him, and that wicked one touches him not.
  -- 1 John 5:18

Be sober; be vigilant: because your adversary the devil, as a roaring lion, walks about, seeking whom he may devour.
  -- 1 Peter 5:8

And that we may be delivered from unreasonable and wicked men, for not all men have faith.
  -- 2 Thessalonians 3:2

For you have been a strength to the poor, a strength to the needy in his distress, a refuge from the storm, a shadow from the heat, when the blast of the terrible ones is as a storm against the wall.
  -- Isaiah 25:4

... Your life is hidden with Christ in God.
  -- Colossians 3:3

Hear my voice, O God, in my prayer; preserve my life from fear of the enemy. Hide me from the secret counsel of the wicked, from the insurrection of the workers of iniquity.
  -- Psalm 64:1, 2

For Loyal Helpers:

... As a son with the father he has served with me in the gospel.
  -- Philippians 2:22

Then the twelve called the multitude of disciples to them and said, "It is not reason that we should leave the word of God and serve tables. Wherefore, brethren, look among you for seven men of honest report, full of the Holy Spirit and wisdom, whom we may appoint over this business."
-- Acts 6:2, 3

Therefore he said to them, "The harvest truly is great, but the laborers are few. Therefore, pray to the Lord of the harvest, that he would send forth laborers into his harvest."
-- Luke 10:2

At my first answer, no man stood with me, but all men forsook me. I pray to God that it may not be laid to their charge.
-- 2 Timothy 4:16

But Moses' hands were heavy; and they took a stone, and put it under him, and he sat on it. And Aaron and Hur held up his hands, the one on one side, and the other on the other side, and his hands were steady until the going down of the sun.
-- Exodus 17:12

And Ittai answered the king and said, "As the LORD lives, and as my lord the king lives, surely in whatever place my lord the king shall be, whether in death or life, even there also will your servant be."
-- 2 Samuel 15:21

That They Would Lead Christ-like Lives

Pray for us, for we trust that we have a good conscience, in all things willing to live honestly.
-- Hebrews 13:18

But you, O man of God, flee these things and follow after righteousness, godliness, faith, love, patience, meekness. Fight the good fight of faith; lay hold on eternal life, whereto you are also called and have professed a good profession before many witnesses.

That you keep this commandment without spot, unrebukable, until the appearing of our Lord Jesus Christ.
     -- 1 Timothy 6:11, 12, 14

... That no man would be able to blame us in this abundance which is administered by us: providing for honest things, not only in the sight of the Lord, but also in the sight of men.
     -- 2 Corinthians 8:20, 21

Abstain from all appearance of evil. And the very God of peace sanctify you wholly, and I pray to God that your whole spirit and soul and body would be preserved blameless unto the coming of our Lord Jesus Christ.
     -- 1 Thessalonians 5:22, 23

According to my earnest expectation and my hope that I shall be ashamed in nothing, but that with all boldness, as always, so now also Christ shall be magnified in my body, whether it be by life or by death.
     -- Philippians 1:20

For this cause we ... do not cease to pray for you and to desire that you might be filled with the knowledge of his will in all wisdom and spiritual understanding; that you might walk worthy of the Lord unto all pleasing, being fruitful in every good work; and increasing in the knowledge of God; strengthened with all might, according to his glorious power, unto all patience and long-suffering with joyfulness.
     -- Colossians 1:9-11

That you may approve things that are excellent; that you may be sincere and without offense until the day of Christ; being filled with the fruits of righteousness, which are by Jesus Christ, to the glory and praise of God.

-- Philippians 1:10, 11

Relationships

Relationships are a big deal to all of us. They are a big deal to God, too. One of the challenges we face is to keep them in good working order. Most of the following verses talk about how to keep relationships from breaking or what can be done to restore them once they are damaged. Many of them can also be used as a springboard for prayer.

Restoration of Relationships:

And I will restore to you the years that the locust has eaten ....
-- Joel 2:25

Moreover, if your brother trespasses against you, go and tell him his fault between you and him alone. If he hears you, you have gained your brother.
-- Matthew 18:15

... If you bring your gift to the altar, and there remember that your brother has anything against you, leave your gift there before the altar, and go your way; first be reconciled to your brother, and then come and offer your gift.
-- Matthew 5:23,24

And when you stand praying, forgive, if you have anything against anyone, so that your Father also which is in heaven may forgive you your trespasses. But if you do not forgive, neither will your Father who is in heaven forgive your trespasses.
-- Mark 11:25, 26

If it is possible, as much as it lies within you, live peaceably with all men.
-- Romans 12:18

A soft answer turns away wrath, but grievous words stir up anger.
-- Proverbs 15:2

... Love your enemies, bless those who curse you, do good to those who hate you, and pray for those who despitefully use you and persecute you, that you may be the children of your Father who is in heaven ....
-- Matthew 5:44, 45

Finally, be all of one mind, having compassion toward one another. Love as brethren, show pity, be courteous -- not rendering evil for evil or railing for railing, but instead blessing, knowing that you are called thereto, so that you shall inherit a blessing.
-- 1 Peter 3:8, 9

... You ought, rather, to forgive him and comfort him, lest perhaps he would be swallowed up with too much sorrow. Therefore I beseech you that you would confirm your love toward him.
-- 2 Corinthians 2:7, 8

Brethren, if a man is overtaken in a fault, let you who are spiritual restore him in the spirit of meekness, considering yourselves, lest you also should be tempted. Bear one another's burdens, and so fulfill the law of Christ.
-- Galatians 6:1, 2

Set a watch, O LORD, before my mouth; keep the door of my lips.
-- Psalm 141:3

Blessed are the merciful, for they shall obtain mercy.

Blessed are the peacemakers, for they shall be called the children of God.
-- Matthew 5:7, 9

(The following two passages go together, and express God's heart to bring families back together:)

Behold, I will send you Elijah the prophet before the coming of the great and dreadful day of the LORD, and he shall turn the hearts of the fathers to the children, and the hearts of the children to their fathers, lest I come and smite the earth with a curse.
-- Malachi 4:5, 6

And he [John the Baptist] shall go before him [Jesus the Savior] in the spirit of Elijah, to turn the hearts of the fathers to the children, and the disobedient to the just, to make ready a people prepared for the Lord.
-- Luke 1:17

And bring here the fatted calf and kill it, and let us eat and be merry. For this son of mine was dead and is alive again; he was lost and is found. And they began to be merry.
-- Luke 15:23, 24 (See Luke 15:11-32, the prodigal son parable.)

The Marriage Covenant:

And the LORD God said, "It is not good for the man to be alone; I will make him a helper suitable for him."
  -- Genesis 2:18

For this cause shall a man leave his father and mother and cleave to his wife, and they two shall be one flesh. So then, they are no more two, but one flesh. Therefore, what God has joined together let man not put asunder [separate].
  -- Mark 10:7-9 (See also Mark 10:1-12 and Matthew 19:1-9.)

… Teach the young women to be sober [seriously minded], to love their husbands, to love their children, to be discreet, chaste, keepers at home, good, obedient to their own husbands, so that the word of God will not be blasphemed.
  -- Titus 2:4, 5

Wives, submit yourselves to your own husbands, as to the Lord. For the husband is the head of the wife, even as Christ is the head of the church …. Therefore, as the church is subject to Christ, so let the wives be to their own husbands in everything.
  -- Ephesians 5:22-24

Husbands, love your wives, even as Christ also loved the church and gave himself for it.
So ought men to love their wives as their own bodies. He who loves his wife loves himself.
  -- Ephesians 5:25, 28

... Let every one of you in particular so love his wife even as himself; and let the wife see to it that she reverences her husband.
— Ephesians 5:33 (See all of Ephesians 5:21-33.)

... Husbands, dwell with [your wives] according to knowledge, giving honor to the wife, as to the weaker vessel, and as being heirs together of the grace of life, so that your prayers are not hindered.
— 1 Peter 3:7 (See all of 1 Peter 3:1-7.)

And to the married I command (yet not I, but the Lord), let the wife not depart from her husband. But if she departs, let her remain unmarried or be reconciled to her husband. And let the husband not divorce his wife.
— 1 Corinthians 7:10 (See all of 1 Corinthians 7:10-16.)

Marriage as a Spiritual Warfare Unit for Kingdom Advance:

So God created man in his own image, in the image of God he created him; male and female he created them. And God blessed them, and God said to them, "Be fruitful, and multiply, and replenish the earth, and subdue it: and have dominion over the fish of the sea, and over the fowl of the air, and over every living thing that moves upon the earth."
— Genesis 1:27, 28

... If two of you shall agree on earth as touching anything that they shall ask, it shall be done for them by my Father who is in heaven. For where two or three are gathered together in my name, there I am in the midst of them.
— Matthew 18:19, 20

Two are better than one, because they have a good reward for their labor. For if one of them falls, the other will lift him up. But woe to him who is alone when he falls, for he does not have another to help him up.

And if one prevails against him, two shall withstand him; and a threefold cord is not quickly broken.

    -- Ecclesiastes 4:9, 10, 12

... Being heirs together of the grace of life, so that your prayers are not hindered.

    -- 1 Peter 3:7

Those Desiring a Marriage Partner:

Whoever finds a wife finds a good thing and obtains favor of the LORD.

    -- Proverbs 18:22

... A prudent wife is from the LORD.

    -- Proverbs 19:14

And the LORD God said, "It is not good that the man should be alone; I will make him a helper suitable for him."

    -- Genesis 2:18

Marriage is honorable in all, and let the bed not be defiled; but fornicators and adulterers God will judge.

    -- Hebrews 13:4

Do not be unequally yoked together with unbelievers. For what fellowship does righteousness have with unrighteousness? And what communion does light have with darkness?

    -- 2 Corinthians 6:14

Children:

Children, obey your parents in the Lord, for this is right. Honor your father and mother, which is the first commandment with promise, so that it may be well with you, and you may live long on the earth.
-- Ephesians 6:1-3

Children, obey your parents in all things, for this is well-pleasing to the Lord.
-- Colossians 3:20

My son, hear the instruction of your father, and do not forsake the law of your mother, for they shall be an ornament of grace to your head and chains about your neck.
-- Proverbs 1:8, 9

Listen to your father who sired you, and do not despise your mother when she is old.
-- Proverbs 23:22

And you fathers, do not provoke your children to wrath, but bring them up in the nurture and admonition of the Lord.
-- Ephesians 6:4

Fathers, do not provoke your children to anger, lest they should be discouraged.
-- Colossians 3:21

Correct your son, and he shall give you rest; yes, he shall give delight to your soul.
-- Proverbs 29:17

Look, children are a heritage of the LORD, and the fruit of the womb is his reward. As arrows are in the hand of a mighty man, so are children of the youth. Happy is the man who has his quiver full of them ....
-- Psalm 127:3-5

The Lonely:

God sets the solitary in families ....
-- Psalm 68:6

A man who has friends must show himself friendly: and there is a friend who sticks closer than a brother.
-- Proverbs 18:24

... The poor commits himself to you; you are the helper of the fatherless.
-- Psalm 10:14

Can a woman forget her nursing child, that she should not have compassion on the son of her womb? Yes, they may forget, yet I will not forget you.
-- Isaiah 49:15

The Barren:

Nothing shall cast its young, nor be barren, in your land: the number of your days I will fulfill.
-- Exodus 23:26

You shall be blessed above all people. There shall not be male or female barren among you or among your cattle.
-- Deuteronomy 7:14

Your wife shall be as a fruitful vine by the sides of your house, your children like olive plants around your table. Behold that thus shall the man be blessed who fears the Lord.
-- Psalm 128:3, 4

He makes the barren woman to keep house and to be a joyful mother of children. Praise the LORD.
-- Psalm 113:9

And Isaac entreated the LORD for his wife, because she was barren, and the LORD was entreated of him, and Rebekah his wife conceived.
-- Genesis 25:21

And God remembered Rachel, and God hearkened to her and opened her womb.
-- Genesis 30:22

And she was in bitterness of soul, and prayed to the LORD, and wept sorely. And she vowed a vow and said, "O LORD of hosts, if you will indeed look on the affliction of your handmaid, and remember me, and not forget your handmaid, but will give to your handmaid a man-child, then I will give him to the LORD all the days of his life ...."

Then Eli answered and said, "Go in peace: and the God of Israel grant you your petition that you have asked of him." ... So the woman went her way, and ate, and her countenance was not sad anymore.

... And the LORD remembered her. ... She bore a son and called his name Samuel, saying, "Because I have asked him of the LORD."
-- 1 Samuel 1:10, 11; 17, 18; 19, 20 (Hannah's story)

The Church

The Church: Christ's beautiful bride. It is popular today among many Christians to scorn and speak evil of the Church, out of disappointment in the worldliness and hypocrisy that is seen among so many of those who call themselves believers. We must not do that, for it grieves the heart of God, Who loves the Church so sacrificially. We must never forget, also, that we ourselves are part of that same Church we may be tempted to speak against.

What would God have us do instead? We can pray for our fellow believers, both individually and corporately, to be the people that God wants us to be. As we pray positively for the Church, we will come to see her through the eyes of Jesus, full of love and compassion. We will become her advocate, cheering her on to excellence and greater Christ-likeness.

Here are some verses which will help you to pray as Jesus would pray for His beloved bride:

For Unity:

A new commandment I give to you, that you love one another: as I have loved you, that you also love one another. By this shall all men know that you are my disciples, if you have love toward each other.
    -- John 13:34, 35

That they all may be one -- as you, Father, are in me, and I am in you, that they also may be one in us, so that the world may believe that you have sent me.
    -- John 17:21

With all lowliness and meekness, with long-suffering, forbearing with each other in love, endeavoring to keep the unity of the Spirit in the bond of peace.
-- Ephesians 4:2, 3

That there should be no schism in the body, but that the members should have the same care one for another. And if one member suffers, all the members suffer with it; or if one member is honored, all the members rejoice with it.
-- 1 Corinthians 12:25, 26 (See all of 1 Corinthians 12:4-27.)

... Be at peace among yourselves.
-- 1 Thessalonians 5:13

Let nothing be done through strife or vain glorying in self, but in lowliness of mind let each esteem the others as better than themselves. Let each of you look out not only for his own things, but every man also for the things of others. Let this mind be in you, which was also in Christ Jesus.
-- Philippians 2:3-5

Now I beseech you, brethren, by the name of our Lord Jesus Christ, that you all speak the same thing and that there be no divisions among you, but that you be perfectly joined together in the same mind and in the same judgment.
-- 1 Corinthians 1:10

For Her Purity:

And may the very God of peace sanctify you wholly, and I pray to God that your whole spirit and soul and body will be preserved blameless unto the coming of our Lord Jesus Christ.
-- 1 Thessalonians 5:23

... Christ also loved the church and gave himself for it, that he might sanctify and cleanse it with the washing of water by the word, that he might present it to himself a glorious church, not having spot, or wrinkle, or any such thing, but that it should be holy and without blemish.
-- Ephesians 5:25-27

I do not pray that you would take them out of the world, but that you would keep them from the evil. They are not of the world, even as I am not of the world. Sanctify them through your truth: your word is truth.
-- John 17:15-17

Seeing, then, that all these things shall be dissolved, what manner of people ought you to be in all holy conversation and godliness?
Wherefore, beloved, seeing that you look for such things, be diligent that you may be found by him in peace, without spot, and blameless.
-- 2 Peter 3:11, 14

But the fruit of the Spirit is love, joy, peace, long-suffering, gentleness, goodness, faith, meekness, temperance; against such there is no law. And they who are Christ's have crucified the flesh with the affections and lusts thereof.
-- Galatians 5:22-24

And this I pray, that your love may abound yet more and more in knowledge and in all judgment, so that you may approve things that are excellent, and so that you may be sincere and without offense until the day of Christ, being filled with the fruits of righteousness, which are by Jesus Christ, to the glory and praise of God.
-- Philippians 1:9-11

Whoever abides in him does not sin; whoever sins has not seen him, neither has he known him.
-- 1 John 3:6

For Her Victory Here on Earth:

Now the God of hope fill you with all joy and peace in believing, that you may abound in hope through the power of the Holy Spirit.
-- Romans 15:13

Mercy to you, and peace, and love, be multiplied.
-- Jude 2

Wherefore, seeing we also are encompassed with such a great cloud of witnesses, let us lay aside every weight and the sin which so easily besets us, and let us run with patience the race that is set before us, looking to Jesus the author and finisher of our faith ....
-- Hebrews 12:1, 2

Now thanks be to God, who always causes us to triumph in Christ, and who makes manifest the savor of his knowledge by us in every place.
-- 2 Corinthians 2:14

No temptation has overtaken you that is not common to man. But God is faithful, who will not suffer you to be tempted with more than you can handle, but will with the temptation also make a way to escape, that you may be able to bear it.
-- 1 Corinthians 10:13

But thanks be to God, who gives us the victory through our Lord Jesus Christ. Therefore, my beloved brethren, be steadfast, unmovable, always abounding in the work of the Lord, forasmuch as you know that your labor is not in vain in the Lord.

    -- 1 Corinthians 15:57, 58

No, in all these things we are more than conquerors through him who loved us.

    -- Romans 8:37

You are of God, little children, and have overcome them, because greater is he who is in you than he who is in the world.

    -- 1 John 4:4

For whatever is born of God overcomes the world, and this is the victory that overcomes the world, even our faith. Who is he who overcomes the world, but he who believes that Jesus is the Son of God?

    -- 1 John 5:4, 5

Her Glorious Future:

Beloved, now we are the sons of God, and it does not yet appear what we shall be. But we know that, when he shall appear, we shall be like him, for we shall see him as he is.

    -- 1 John 3:2

And I John saw the holy city, new Jerusalem, coming down from God out of heaven, prepared as a bride adorned for her husband.

    -- Revelation 21:2

And there came to me one of the seven angels which had the seven vials full of the seven last plagues, and talked with me, saying, "Come here; I will show you the bride, the Lamb's wife." And he carried me away in the spirit to a great and high mountain, and showed me that great city, the holy Jerusalem, descending out of heaven from God, having the glory of God. And her light was like a stone most precious, even like a jasper stone, clear as crystal.

-- Revelations 21:9-11

For our conversation is in heaven, from where we also look for the Savior, the Lord Jesus Christ, who shall change our vile [lowly] body, that it may be fashioned to be like his glorious body, according to the working by which he is able even to subdue all things to himself.

-- Philippians 3:20, 21

But the saints of the Most High shall take the kingdom and possess the kingdom forever, even forever and ever.

Until the Ancient of Days came, and judgment was given to the saints of the Most High, and the time came that the saints possessed the kingdom.

-- Daniel 7:18, 22

And behold, I come quickly, and my reward is with me, to give every man according to how his work shall be. I am Alpha and Omega, the beginning and the end, the first and the last.

He who testifies these things says, "Surely I come quickly. Amen." Even so, come, Lord Jesus.

-- Revelation 22:12, 13, 20

Our Final Assurance

God Always Knew It All

It is a comfort to our hearts, when we are thrown a curve ball, to know that nothing that happens ever takes God by surprise. He sits above time, viewing the entire past through the entire future all at the same time.

Because He knows what lies ahead for us, He has planned for it and has put help and provision in place for us. He doesn't have to suddenly come up with a new strategy when things seem to go awry. It is already taken care of, and we can rest as we look to Him for His solutions to whatever we face.

These Scriptures will help you have confidence that God has everything well under control:

Declaring the end from the beginning, and from ancient times the things that are not yet done, saying, "My counsel shall stand, and I will do all my pleasure. ... Yes, I have spoken it; I will also bring it to pass. I have purposed it; I will also do it."
-- Isaiah 46:10, 11

Behold, the former things have now come to pass, and new things I declare: before they spring forth I tell you of them.
-- Isaiah 42:9

...Who has declared this from ancient time? Who has told it from that time? Have not I, the LORD? And there is no other God beside me ....
-- Isaiah 45:21

Great is our Lord and of great power. His understanding is infinite.
-- Psalm 147:5

For the word of God is … a discerner of the thoughts and intents of the heart. Neither is there any creature that is hidden from his sight, but all things are naked and opened to the eyes of him with whom we have to do.
-- Hebrews 4:12, 13

… He who teaches man knowledge, shall he not know?
-- Psalm 94:10

Why, *seeing times are not hidden from the Almighty*, do they who know him not see his days?
-- Job 24:1 (Italics mine)

O LORD, you have searched me and known me. You know when I sit down and when I arise; you understand my thought afar off.
-- Psalm 139:1, 2

I have declared the former things from the beginning, and they went forth from my mouth, and I showed them. I did them suddenly, and they came to pass.
I have even from the beginning declared it to you; before it came to pass I showed it to you …. I have showed you new things from this time, even hidden things, and you did not know them.
-- Isaiah 48:3, 5, 6

… For Jesus knew from the beginning who they were who did not believe and who would betray him.
-- John 6:64

... For he knows the secrets of the heart.
    -- Psalm 44:21

... [God] has determined the times already appointed and the bounds of their habitation.
    -- Acts 17:26

[Jesus], being delivered by the determinate counsel *and foreknowledge of God*, you have taken and by wicked hands have crucified and slain.
    -- Acts 2:23 (Italics mine)

God Ultimately Will Have His Way

It would be wonderful if people always cooperated with God and did their part to advance His will in the earth. God has given mankind the freedom to move with Him or at cross-purposes to His plan, and in a fallen world, we see the problems that this freewill privilege can cause.

However, in the big picture, in spite of man's poor choices, God still somehow sees to it that His will is accomplished overall. He may have to use different people than those He originally called to get the job done, and the timeframe may seem to be delayed, but He will still make sure His plan succeeds. As we saw in our last chapter, He always knew it would pan out the way it does anyway.

What does this mean for us individually? We need never fear that God's purposes for our personal lives can be thwarted by other people. As long as we are faithful, God will move us into the destiny for which He has created us. He has everything well in hand for us individually, for our loved ones, and for the world as a whole.

When you are tempted to doubt whether God's plan will come to fruition, meditate on these verses to restore your confidence:

In whom also we have obtained an inheritance, being predestinated according to the purpose of him who works all things after the counsel of his own will.
-- Ephesians 1:11

I know that you can do everything, and that no thought can be withheld from you.
-- Job 42:2

I know that you can do all things; no plan of yours can be thwarted.
-- Job 42:2 (NIV)

Declaring the end from the beginning and from ancient times the things that are not yet done, saying, "My counsel shall stand, and I will do all my pleasure. ... Yes, I have spoken it; I will also bring it to pass. I have purposed it; I will also do it."
-- Isaiah 46:10, 11

There are many devices in a man's heart; nevertheless, the counsel of the LORD, that shall stand.
-- Proverbs 19:21

Many are the plans in a man's heart, but it is the LORD's purpose that prevails.
-- Proverbs 19:21 (NIV)

There is neither wisdom, nor understanding, nor counsel against the LORD.
-- Proverbs 21:30

There is no wisdom, no insight, no plan that can succeed against the LORD.
-- Proverbs 21:30 (NIV)

Who is he who speaks and it comes to pass, when the Lord has not commanded it?
-- Lamentations 3:37

The LORD brings the counsel of the heathen to naught; he makes the devices of the people of no effect. The counsel of the LORD stands forever, the thoughts of his heart to all generations.
-- Psalm 33:10, 11

The LORD of hosts has sworn, saying, "Surely as I have thought, so shall it come to pass, and as I have purposed, so shall it stand."
For the LORD of hosts has purposed, and who shall disannul it? And his hand is stretched out, and who shall turn it back?
-- Isaiah 14:24, 27

But our God is in the heavens: he has done whatever he has pleased.
-- Psalm 115:3

But he [God] is in one mind, and who can turn him? And what his soul desires, even that he does. For he performs the thing that is appointed for me, and many such things are with him.
-- Job 23:13, 14

The Battle Is the Lord's

Intercessors understand that receiving our answers to prayer involves battle. But sometimes we focus too much on the spiritual conflict we are engaged in, and our perspective begins to skew. When that happens, we can become discouraged, spiritually unhealthy -- even deceived.

We must learn to keep our eyes steadily fixed on Jesus, rather than the war going on around us, or we become darkened. This is not His will for His beloved intercessors. If our attention is fastened on Jesus above all else, we will be light-filled, no matter what we have to pray into. It is not an easy task to keep our focus in line, but if we continuously remind ourselves that the battle is His, not ours, we will be all right.

Many of us must learn to stop striving in our own flesh for those prayer victories, and let the Holy Spirit fuel our prayers. The battle truly is up to the Lord. Rather than wearing ourselves out, praying from a place of thinking success or defeat all hangs on us, we must learn to cooperate with Him and confidently rest in knowing that He will fight for us. This is the place of abiding. Moses, David, Jehoshaphat, and Elisha all found it, and we can, too.

Meditating on these verses will help you shake off futile striving, so that you can enter into the victory the Lord intends for you:

And they were helped against them ... for they cried to God in the battle, and he was entreated of them -- because they put their trust in him.
-- 1 Chronicles 5:20

For the eyes of the LORD run to and fro throughout the whole earth, to show himself strong on behalf of those whose hearts are perfect toward him.

-- 2 Chronicles 16:9

... This is what the LORD says to you: "Do not be afraid or dismayed by reason of this great multitude: for the battle is not yours, but God's."

-- 2 Chronicles 20:15

... Fear not. Stand still, and see the salvation of the LORD, which he will show to you today: for the Egyptians whom you have seen today, you shall see them again no more forever. The LORD shall fight for you, and you shall hold your peace.

-- Exodus 14:13, 14

Now thanks be to God, who always causes us to triumph in Christ ....

-- 2 Corinthians 2:14

And Asa cried to the LORD his God, and said, "LORD, it is not hard at all for you to help, whether with many, or with those who have no power. Help us, O LORD our God, for we rest on you, and in your name we go against this multitude. O LORD, you are our God; do not let man prevail against you."

-- 2 Chronicles 14:11

Through God we shall do valiantly, for it is he who shall trample down our enemies.

-- Psalm 60:12

He has delivered my soul in peace from the battle that was against me: for there were many with me.

-- Psalm 55:18

... Our God shall fight for us.
    -- Nehemiah 4:20

For the LORD has driven out from before you great and strong nations: but as for you, no man has been able to stand before you to this day. One man of you shall chase a thousand: for the LORD your God is he who fights for you, as he has promised you.
    -- Joshua 23:9, 10

You shall not fear them, for the LORD your God shall fight for you.
    -- Deuteronomy 3:22

The LORD is on my side; I will not fear. What can man do to me? The LORD takes my part with those who help me: therefore shall I see my desire upon them who hate me.
    -- Psalm 118:6, 7

And all this assembly shall know that the LORD does not save with sword and spear, for the battle is the LORD's, and he will give you into our hands.
    -- 1 Samuel 17:47

... Not by might, nor by power, but by my Spirit, says the LORD of hosts.
    -- Zechariah 4:6

With him is an arm of flesh, but with us is the LORD our God to help us and to fight our battles.
    -- 2 Chronicles 32:8

When you go out to battle against your enemies and see horses, and chariots, and a people more than you, do not be afraid of them: for the LORD your God is with you, who brought you up out of the land of Egypt. And it shall be, when you come near to the battle ... do not let your hearts faint, do not fear, and do not tremble, neither be terrified because of them: for the LORD your God is he who goes with you, to fight for you against your enemies, to save you.

  -- Deuteronomy 20:1-4

And when the servant of the man of God had arisen early and gone forth, behold, a host surrounded the city, both with horses and chariots. And his servant said to him, "Alas, my master! What shall we do?" And he answered, "Fear not: for they who are with us are more than they who are with them." And Elisha prayed and said, "LORD, I ask you to open his eyes, so that he may see." And the LORD opened the young man's eyes, and he saw. And behold, the mountain was full of horses and chariots of fire round about Elisha.

  -- 2 Kings 6:15-17

For though we walk in the flesh, we do not war after the flesh (for the weapons of our warfare are not carnal [soulish], but mighty *through God* to the pulling down of strongholds).

  -- 2 Corinthians 10: 3, 4 (Italics mine)

For they did not get possession of the land by their own sword; neither did their own arm save them. It was by your right hand, and your arm, and the light of your countenance, because you had favor toward them.

  -- Psalm 44:3

In God We Have Ultimate Victory

Although we may get weary along the way, God's promise is sure: He will give us the victory in the end. Our assignment is to persevere in prayer and in other well-doing, to not give up, and to place all our confidence in Him. *Never* accept defeat. Setbacks there will be, but God promises victory to those who will endure.

You will see the obtainment of many things for which you have battled in prayer in this life, but some of your conquests will manifest themselves only after you have gone on to be with the Lord. Your prayers live on and on, and are never forgotten before the throne.

The greatest victory you will ever obtain is to finish your life-course well, having been firm in your faith and your allegiance to Jesus until the end.

Do not rejoice against me, O my enemy. When I fall, I shall arise; when I sit in darkness, the LORD shall be a light to me.
-- Micah 7:8

Now thanks be to God, who always causes us to triumph in Christ ....
-- 2 Corinthians 2:14

Through God we shall do valiantly, for it is he who shall trample down our enemies.
-- Psalm 60:12

For whatever is born of God overcomes the world. And this is the victory that overcomes the world, even our faith. Who is he who overcomes the world? He who believes that Jesus is the Son of God.
-- 1 John 5:4, 5

And what is the exceeding greatness of his power toward us who believe, according to the working of his mighty power, which he wrought in Christ, when he raised him from the dead and set him at his own right hand in the heavenly places, far above all principality, and power, and might, and dominion, and every name that is named -- not only in this world, but also in that which is to come -- and has put all things under his feet ....
-- Ephesians 1:19-22

But thanks be to God, who gives us the victory through our Lord Jesus Christ.
-- 1 Corinthians 15:57

And having spoiled principalities and powers, he made a show of them openly, triumphing over them in it.
-- Colossians 2:13

No, in all these things we are more than conquerors through him who loved us. For I am persuaded that neither death, nor life, nor angels, nor principalities, nor powers, nor things present, nor things to come, nor height, nor depth, nor any other creature, shall be able to separate us from the love of God, which is in Christ Jesus our Lord.
-- Romans 8:37-39

And they overcame him by the blood of the Lamb and by the word of their testimony, and they did not love their lives, even unto the death.

    -- Revelation 12:11

Appendices

Appendix A

Decreeing the Will of God

It has been said that prayer brings what has been legislated in heaven down into the earth. One of the ways we do that is through the decree.

There are many variations on intercessory prayer: petition, thanksgiving, and the prayer of faith, for instance. Decreeing has become popular in recent years, but I see that there has been some abuse. In spite of the teaching surrounding it, you cannot decree something just because you think it is a good idea and have it happen.

In 1 Kings 17:1, when Elijah stood before King Ahab and declared, "*As the LORD God of Israel lives, before whom I stand, there shall not be dew or rain these years, except according to my word,*" he was not speaking from his own idea of what should be done. "Before whom I stand" indicates that he was standing in the counsel and authority of the Lord. James 5:16, 17 reveals to us that before Elijah decreed the drought, he had been in earnest prayer leading up to it. The decree should never be taken lightly or done without the unction of the Spirit.

What is true decreeing, then? A decree (sometimes called a proclamation or a declaration) calls forth the will of God the Father by firmly speaking that a particular thing shall happen. It speaks into existence the purpose of God. It is usually a one-time statement of what shall be, done in the anointing of a Holy Spirit-given moment or by direct commandment of the Lord, with all the authority of heaven backing it. It is actually a form of prophecy. The prayer warrior speaking the decree understands that he or she is the mouthpiece of God in that moment, declaring His purpose in the Name of Jesus, and that what is being spoken shall certainly come to pass.

The following verses either speak of the decree or will help you understand the elements of decreeing:

You shall also decree a thing, and it shall be established to you, and the light shall shine upon your ways.
-- Job 22:28

… Even God, who quickens [makes alive] the dead and calls those things which are not as though they were.
-- Romans 4:17

Jesus answered and said to them, "Truly I say to you, if you have faith and do not doubt, … if you shall say to this mountain, 'Be removed, and be cast into the sea,' it shall be done."
-- Matthew 21:21 (Read Matthew 21:18-21, an example of Jesus using the decree.)

I believed, therefore have I spoken ….
-- Psalm 116:10

… He has made a decree which shall not pass.
-- Psalm 148:6 (Agree with God by decreeing what He decrees.)

Who is he who says, and it comes to pass, when the Lord does not command it?
-- Lamentations 3:37

If any man speaks, let him speak as the oracles of God ….
-- 1 Peter 4:11

Appendix B

Spiritual Warfare

As intercessors, most of us are keenly aware that receiving needed prayer answers often involves spiritual warfare. I could not conclude *The Intercessor's Companion* without a few further words on this important subject.

For too long, we intercessors have been focusing on the darkness that we contend against, rather than focusing on Jesus, our Light. When we keep our eyes on our Commander-in-Chief, rather than focusing on the enemy, we stay strong and victorious for the battle. Our lives mirror and radiate whatever we are looking at. Keep your joy; keep your strength; keep your hope firmly fastened in Jesus, your unshakable Deliverer. (For an in-depth look at spiritual warfare, please see my book, *The Intercessor Manual*, available at our website, FullGospelFamily.com.)

The Psalms are a wonderful warfare manual. David was a warrior, and he knew how to fight his battles in the Lord's anointing. Psalms 91, 34, and 23 are particularly significant to me in keeping steady and standing my ground.

Jesus has already provided for your total victory through His finished work at the cross. This means that whatever you are praying for while standing on true biblical ground can be yours. You must simply stay at it, enforcing the victory already won by our Lord.

Here are a few more Scripture verses to assist you toward winning the war:

... Now salvation, and strength, and the kingdom of our God have come, and the power of his Christ: for the accuser of our brethren is cast down, which accused them before our God day and night. And they overcame him by the blood of the Lamb and by the word of their testimony, and they did not love their lives, even unto the death. Therefore, rejoice, you heavens, and you that dwell in them ....
    -- Revelation 12:10-12

... For you have magnified your word above all your name. In the day when I cried, you answered me and strengthened me with strength in my soul.
    -- Psalm 138:2, 3

Forever, O LORD, your word is settled in heaven.
    -- Psalm 119:89

For whatever is born of God overcomes the world, and this is the victory that overcomes the world, even our faith. Who is he who overcomes the world, but he who believes that Jesus is the Son of God?
    -- 1 John 5:4, 5

Therefore let no man glory in men, for all things are yours ... and you are Christ's, and Christ is God's.
    -- 1 Corinthians 3:21, 23

You, therefore, endure hardness, as a good soldier of Jesus Christ. No man who wars entangles himself with the affairs of this life, so that he may please him who has chosen him to be a soldier.
    -- 2 Timothy 2:3, 4

For though we walk in the flesh, we do not war after the flesh (for the weapons of our warfare are not carnal [soulish], but mighty through God to the pulling down of strongholds), casting down imaginations and every high thing that exalts itself against the knowledge of God, and bringing into captivity every thought to the obedience of Christ.
> -- 2 Corinthians 10:3-5

And has raised us up together, and made us sit together in heavenly places in Christ Jesus.
> -- Ephesians 2:6 (War from your throne room position downward, enforcing Christ's finished work.)

The night is far spent; the day is at hand. Let us therefore cast off the works of darkness, and let us put on the armor of light.

But put on the Lord Jesus Christ, and do not make provision for the flesh, to fulfill the lusts thereof.
> -- Romans 13:12, 14

Finally, my brethren, be strong in the Lord, and in the power of his might. Put on the whole armor of God, that you may be able to stand against the wiles of the devil.

Wherefore take to yourselves the whole armor of God, that you may be able to withstand in the evil day, and having done all, to stand. Stand therefore ....
> -- Ephesians 6:10-11, 13-14 (See all of Ephesians 6:10-18.)

I have fought a good fight; I have finished my course; I have kept the faith. From this time forth a crown of righteousness is laid up for me, which the Lord, the righteous judge, shall give me at that day -- and not to me only, but to all those who also love his appearing.
> -- 2 Timothy 4:7, 8

Through God we shall do valiantly, for it is he who shall trample down our enemies.

    -- Psalm 60:12

About the Author

Lee Ann Rubsam is an apostolic/prophetic intercessor leader and teacher. Her focus is on encouraging other intercessors in their calling and helping them to reach their highest level of effectiveness in prayer. With that goal in mind, in addition to her books, she and her husband Paul present practical, hands-on intercessor workshops around the nation.

Lee Ann also writes character education materials for home school families, home Bible study groups, and Christian education/discipleship classes within the local church.

For other prayer or Christian character resources, please visit Lee Ann's publishing website, *FullGospelFamily.com*.

For information about hosting an intercessor workshop in your area, visit *OutOfTheFireMinistries.org* or contact Lee Ann at leeann@leeannrubsam.com.

Made in the USA
Lexington, KY
20 December 2012